Inhaltsverzeichnis

D1721026

A A holiday job

1 Simple present

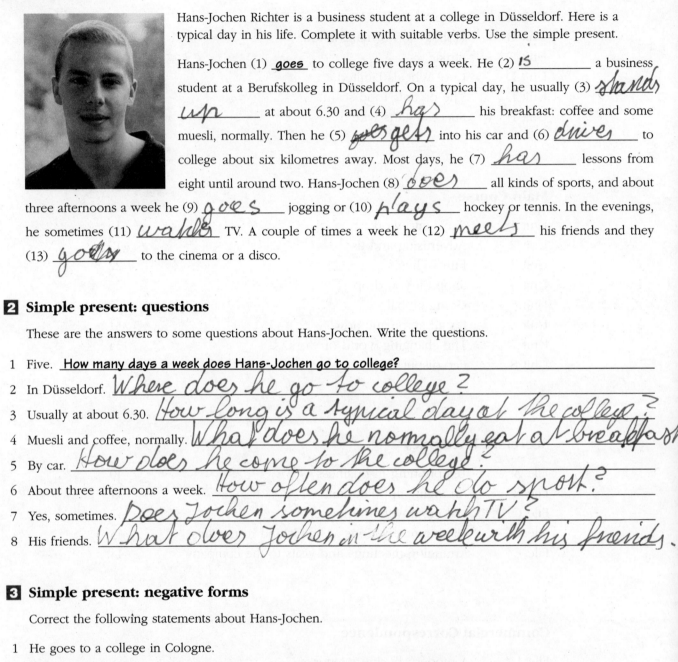

Hans-Jochen Richter is a business student at a college in Düsseldorf. Here is a typical day in his life. Complete it with suitable verbs. Use the simple present.

Hans-Jochen (1) **goes** to college five days a week. He (2) *is* a business student at a Berufskolleg in Düsseldorf. On a typical day, he usually (3) *stands up* at about 6.30 and (4) *has* his breakfast: coffee and some muesli, normally. Then he (5) *goes gets* into his car and (6) *drives* to college about six kilometres away. Most days, he (7) *has* lessons from eight until around two. Hans-Jochen (8) *does* all kinds of sports, and about three afternoons a week he (9) *goes* jogging or (10) *plays* hockey or tennis. In the evenings, he sometimes (11) *watch* TV. A couple of times a week he (12) *meets* his friends and they (13) *goes* to the cinema or a disco.

2 Simple present: questions

These are the answers to some questions about Hans-Jochen. Write the questions.

1 Five. **How many days a week does Hans-Jochen go to college?**
2 In Düsseldorf. *Where does he go to college?*
3 Usually at about 6.30. *How long is a typical day at the college?*
4 Muesli and coffee, normally. *What does he normally eat at breakfast*
5 By car. *How does he come to the college?*
6 About three afternoons a week. *How often does he do sport?*
7 Yes, sometimes. *Does Jochen sometimes watch TV?*
8 His friends. *What does Jochen in the week with his friends.*

3 Simple present: negative forms

Correct the following statements about Hans-Jochen.

1 He goes to a college in Cologne.

   He doesn't go to a college in Cologne. He goes to a college in Düsseldorf.

2 He normally eats toast for breakfast.
   He doesn't eat toast for breakfast. He eats muesli.

3 He rides his bicycle to college.
   He doesn't rides his bicycle to college. He drives with his c

4 He plays football in the afternoon.
   He doesn't play football in the afternoon. He plays hockey or tenny.

5 Hans-Jochen and his friends go to the theatre in the evenings.
   They doesn't go to thatre. they go to ll cinema or in the Disco

4 Present continuous

It is the middle of August and Hans-Jochen is not at college – and not doing any of the things that he normally does. He is in England with the Living World organization. He is phoning an English friend in London. Write in the correct forms of the verbs (present continuous).

HANS-JOCHEN	Hi, Charlie. It's Hans-Jochen.
CHARLIE	Hans-Jochen! Great to hear from you. Are you in Düsseldorf?
HANS-JOCHEN	No, I (1) __am ringing__ (ring) from England. I (2) _am spending_ (spend) five weeks on Dartmoor at the moment.
CHARLIE	On Dartmoor? What on earth (3) _are you doing_ (you / do) there?
HANS-JOCHEN	I (4) _am making_ (make) footpaths, if you can believe that. There's this organization called Living World that employs students from all over the world. I'm, well, part of a team that (5) _is working_ (work) on a project on Dartmoor.
CHARLIE	Sounds like hard work to me!
HANS-JOCHEN	It's not too bad. The best thing is that the other fourteen students in the team come from lots of different countries, so I (6) _am speaking_ (speak) a lot of English at the moment.
CHARLIE	So where (7) _are you staying_ (you / stay) while you're here?
HANS-JOCHEN	Well, most of the groups usually stay in youth hostels, but we (8) _aren't doing / do not_ (not / do) that. I'm not sure why. We (9) _are staying_ (stay) in a hotel. It's great. Your own room. A bar and billiards in the evenings …
CHARLIE	Any chance that you can come to London some time?
HANS-JOCHEN	I'd love to, Charlie. I'll have a couple of days free at the end. I could come then …

5 Simple present, present continuous

Here is a local newspaper article from the *Dartmoor Echo*. Complete it with the correct forms of the verbs: simple present or present continuous.

Building footpaths – and bridges

Fifteen overseas students (1) __are__ (be) busy on Dartmoor this summer helping to keep Britain's most famous National Park beautiful for visitors.

The students, who (2) _come_ (come) from Germany, France, the Netherlands and Sweden, (3) _are making_ (make) footpaths. They (4) _are_ (be) here with Living World, an organization that (5) _specializes_ (specialize) in nature conservation.

'It (6) _is_ (be) hard work,' said 18-year-old Annik Le Meur from Brittany, 'but we (7) _love_ (love) being here on Dartmoor.

The days (8) _seem_ (seem) to go very quickly.'

The other students (9) _are thinking / think_ (think) the same. 'I normally just (10) _sit_ (sit) at home and (11) _do_ (do) nothing during the summer holidays,' said Lars Bergenssen from Sweden. 'But here I (12) _am getting_ (get) very fit, and I (13) _am meeting_ (meet) lots of new people.'

For the students, working on Dartmoor (14) _is meaning / means_ (mean) not only building footpaths, but also building bridges – between nations.

B *Holiday job or hard labour?*

1 Past continuous

Claire works in the personnel department *(Personalabteilung)* of an insurance company.
This was the scene in her office yesterday when she arrived at work at about 8.30. What was everyone doing?
Write five sentences using the phrases below and the past continuous.

> to write a letter ■ to talk to (someone) ■ to phone (someone) ■ to read a newspaper
> ■ to photocopy documents ■ to water (the plants)

EXAMPLE **Bill was reading a newspaper.**   3 Andrea _____

1 Nicky _____   4 Mike _____

2 Tony _____   5 Lynn _____

2 Past continuous: questions

Make questions about Claire's office.

EXAMPLE (newspaper / read / who) **Who was reading a newspaper?** _____

1 (Nicky / do / what) _____

2 (Tony / phone / who) _____

3 (Andrea / talk / the computer technician / why) _____

4 (Mike / photocopy / what) _____

5 (her plants / water / who) _____

3 Simple past

Fill in the simple past forms of the verbs in brackets.

Claire is 22 years old, and the job at the insurance company is her first job. This is how she got here.

She (1) __finished__ (finish) school when she was 18. She (2) _____ (know) that she

(3) _____ (want) to go to business college, but she (4) _____ (not / want) to

go there directly after school. 'I want to do something different first,' she (5) _____ (tell) her

friends and family. She (6) _____ (decide) to work for a year between school and college.

One morning, about two months later, Claire (7) _____ (wake up) in Los Angeles, in the

(very rich!) family of a Hollywood film producer. She (8) _____ (be) an au pair.

Claire really (9) _____ (love) her year in the United States. The two children in the family

(10) _____ (be) terrible but Claire still (11) _____ (have) a great time.

The work (12) _____ (not / be) too hard. She (13) _____ (swim) in the

pool every afternoon and (14) _____ (drink) Martinis on the terrace every evening.

Sometimes she even (15) _____ (get) the chance to go to the film studios with Larry, where

she (16) _____ (meet) some of her favourite actors. She (17) _____ (learn)

a lot about herself that year, too and really (18) _____ (grow up).

When she was back in Britain, she (19) _____ (do) her business course at college.

She (20) _____ (find) personnel work particularly interesting. Just before the end of the

course she (21) _____ (see) an advertisement in the newspaper for the job at the insurance

company. She (22) _____ (ring) the company, (23) _____ (go) for an

interview – and they (24) _____ (give) her the job.

4 Simple past: mixed forms

Claire and her friend Ann are talking about Claire's year in America. Cross out the incorrect verbs.

1 Ann: Tell me, what ... about America?

   liked you / didn't you like / did you not liked

2 Claire: Well, the children, yes, the children ... terrible, awful!

   were / was / weren't

3 Claire: They ... what I said.

   didn't do / did not / did not did

4 Claire: And they were so lazy. For example, they ... their beds.
   No, never!

   made no / didn't made / didn't make

5 Claire: And the washing up – of course they ... me with that.

   not helped / help / didn't help

6 Ann: So ... any fun with the children?

   have you / did you have / do you have

7 Claire: Oh yes, the best fun I ... was when they were asleep in bed!

   didn't have / did / had

5 Simple past, past continuous

Make sentences. Use the word in brackets.

EXAMPLES Claire / sit / at her desk / the phone / ring (when)

Claire was sitting at her desk when the phone rang.

they / talk / the boss / come in (while)

While they were talking, the boss came in.

1 Claire / live / in the US / she / often / visit / the film studios (while)

_____

2 she / visit / the studios / one day / Leonardo di Caprio / speak to her (when)

_____

3 she / study / at college / she / become / interested in personnel work (while)

_____

4 she / read / the newspaper / one day / she / see / the advertisement (while)

_____

5 Claire / sit / in the garden at home / the firm / phone / to tell / her / she had the job (when)

_____

6 Crossword

Complete the crossword with the simple past forms of the verbs.

Across

1 see
5 open
7 drink
8 let
10 become
11 look
15 agree
16 eat
17 write

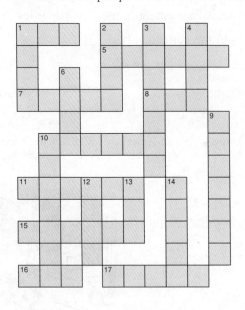

Down

1 say
2 take
3 reply
4 go
6 give
9 plan
10 bring
12 know
13 do
14 build

7 Words!

What are the missing words? Look in Unit B in your textbook.

1 Many young people take a **y**_____ **o**_____ between school and college or work.

2 Simon Carr worked as a **w**_____ while he was in Italy.

3 I wanted some time to go sightseeing, so I only took a **p**_____ **-t**_____ job.

4 Working abroad can be good **t**_____ for later life.

5 If you work as an **a**_____ **p**_____ , you might have to look after awful children.

6 Anika had to work hard, but she thought that the **p**_____ was fair.

C *Strike!*

1 Simple present, simple past, present perfect

Here is some more information about Josh, Carol and the disco where they work. In each group of three sentences, one verb is in the simple present, one in the simple past and one in the present perfect. Which is which? Write in the correct forms of the verbs in brackets.

1 a The Rock Palace __is__ (be) in Manchester.

   b It __opened__ (open) three years ago.

   c It _____ (exist) for three years.

2 a Josh _____ (work) at the disco since it began.

   b He _____ (work) in the bar now.

   c His first job _____ (be) selling tickets at the door.

3 a Carol _____ (come) here directly after leaving school.

   b She _____ (work) at the Rock Palace for about six months.

   c She _____ (be) a good friend of Josh's.

4 a The disco _____ (belong) to a man called Benny.

   b Benny _____ (open) his first small club in Manchester in 1991.

   c Since then, he _____ (open) five discos, three bars, a restaurant and a casino.

5 a The Rock Palace _____ (become) Manchester's most popular disco in recent years.

   b Lots of young people _____ (come) to the club every evening.

   c Over a thousand _____ (come) yesterday evening alone.

2 Present perfect, simple past: signal words

In the puzzle, there are fourteen signal words that you often use with the simple past / present perfect. Write them into the correct lists. (Tip: some words are diagonal.)

| O N M O N D A Y K V |
| T Y U J L A T E L Y |
| F S E U N E N K L U |
| O B B S R X E Y Z S |
| R Y E T T E V E R I |
| J A C S W E E R X N |
| M W G T Y N R T I C |
| N O S O F A R D Q E |
| L A L W A Y S Q A Z |
| L U F A L R E A D Y |

SIMPLE PAST	PRESENT PERFECT
on Monday	

3 Present perfect, simple past

Nick and Karen work in a Fitness Club next door to the Rock Palace. Look at this conversation which contains the signal words from the word puzzle and fill in the simple past or present perfect.

NICK   Hi, Karen. How are you this morning?

KAREN   Tired! I (1) __was__ (be) at a party yesterday evening and (2) _____ (not / get) home till four.

NICK   I know the feeling. Sorry, but we need to talk about the Open Day next Saturday. Jeff hopes to get lots of new members so we had better organize it really well. You (3) _____ (put) the advertisement about it in the paper last week, didn't you?

KAREN   Yes, on Tuesday.

NICK   (4) _____ (we / have) any phone calls or anything about it yet?

KAREN   Yes, quite a lot of people (5) _____ (already / call) to ask about joining and to say they want to come.

NICK   That's good. Now. What do we need to get? We (6) _____ (never / have) an open day before, so I'm not really sure. Should we get wine as well as water and orange juice?

KAREN   I think so, yes. And maybe some food, too. I (7) _____ (be) to a couple of open days at other clubs recently and they (8) _____ (always / have) a buffet. It makes it much nicer.

NICK   OK, then. Can you buy the things we need?

KAREN   No problem. Where's Jeff, anyway? I (9) _____ (not / see) him for days.

NICK   I think he's on holiday again.

KAREN   On holiday? He's always on holiday! He (10) _____ (take) about three months off so far this year. He (11) _____ (be) in Tunisia only a few weeks ago. But when you're the boss …

4 Words!

Match the words and the definitions. Then use some of the words to complete the sentences.

1	nonsense	a	hours that you work which are extra to your normal hours
2	to walk out	b	something that you win when you are the best, come first in a race, etc
3	to borrow	c	something which is stupid or not logical
4	overtime	d	to go on strike
5	satisfied	e	to get money (eg from a bank) which you have to pay back later
6	customers	f	to use money to pay for something
7	prize	g	you are … when you are happy and feel that everything is OK
8	to finance	h	people who buy something (eg in a shop, from a company, etc)

1 The workers were so unhappy about their wages that they all decided _____ .

2 We are so busy at work at the moment that all of us are having to do _____ every day.

3 I think your idea for a club is great, but how are you going _____ it?

4 The shop is dirty, and the people who work there are mostly unfriendly. The result is that in the last six months they have lost almost all their _____ .

5 Mike. Sometimes you talk complete _____ !

D Cool Wheels Limited

1 Modal verbs

Here are some tips from a leaflet called 'Starting Your Own Small Business'. Read them carefully, then decide if the statements below are true or false.

> ### Five tips for starting your own business
>
> - Think about yourself. Before you begin ask: Am I the right sort of person to run a small business? Can I work alone? Talk to friends and family, too. Running a business *will* be hard work and *will* change your life.
> - Have the skills and knowledge that you need. All sorts of people start businesses, some with formal qualifications, but many also (and very successfully) without. If you decide that you need more training – on computers, for example – go and get it. There are lots of courses that you can go on – and the government will often pay.
> - Know your market. Just because you think your idea is a good one, it does not mean that other people will agree. Before you begin, you need to know your market. Will enough people want your product or service? Who are your competitors? Find out.
> - Have a business plan. Will you need to borrow money from a bank? Make a 'business plan' – for yourself, and if you need a bank behind you, for the bank manager. You will not be able to borrow money without one.
> - Don't give up! Once you begin, don't give up too easily. There *will* be problems in even the best-planned business. If things go wrong, don't panic. Get help if needed. You can succeed!

TRUE OR FALSE?

1 People who want to start their own business must be able to work alone. ☐ t

2 Your life after starting a business might perhaps be very different. ☐ f

3 You have to have formal college qualifications to run your own business. ☐

4 You can get more training if you need it, but you always have to pay for it yourself. ☐

5 You should always find out about your market before you begin. ☐

6 You needn't know about your competitors before you begin. ☐

7 You must make a business plan for yourself, and for the bank if you need to borrow money. ☐

8 You might have problems once you begin. ☐

9 You must panic and give up as soon as you have a problem. ☐

10 If you do all the things in the tips, you can be successful in your own business. ☐

Now rewrite the sentences that are wrong. Use suitable modal verbs (including *will / won't*).

2 <u>Your life after starting a business will definitely be very different.</u>

☐ _____

☐ _____

☐ _____

☐ _____

☐ _____

2 (be) allowed to

The Berkeley's Bank Business Card is a special credit card for people with their own small business.
Here is some information about it. Replace the forms of *can* with (*be) allowed to*.

1 Anyone with a small business who has had a normal Berkeley's account

   (Konto) for six months ~~can~~ __is allowed to__ get the business card.

2 The credit limit is £5,000. That means you can _____

   _____ spend up to £5,000 at any time.

3 With some cards in the past, other people in the company could not

   _____ use the boss's card. The Berkeley's card

   is different: up to four employees can _____ use it, too.

4 The balance on the card has to be paid in full every month. If you do not do this, you will not be able to

   _____ keep your card.

Berkeley's Bank
Business Card

3046 3460 3312

4046   VALID
         THRU 06/00 ✔

BB

3 The future

Some time after his conversation with his grandfather (textbook pages 17–18), Alex meets Pop again in town. Complete what they say with future forms: *will, going to,* the present continuous or the simple present. Where you think that more than one answer is possible, choose the best one. Then tick the table on page 11 to show how you decided.

ALEX   Hey, Pop. How are things?
POP   Oh, hello, Alex. Yes, fine, thanks.
ALEX   Look, thanks a lot for the talk the other day. It was really helpful.
POP   I'm glad. So, what (1) (you / do), then?
ALEX   I (2) (get) some capital, like you said, so that Jeff and I can be real partners, you know, fifty-fifty.

POP   I think that (3) (be) much better. Have you actually done anything about getting some money yet?
ALEX   Yes. I (4) (see) a bank manager next Tuesday morning. I hope she (5) (be able to) help.
POP   Good for you, Alex. How much do you expect you (6) (need)?
ALEX   Ten, fifteen thousand maybe.
POP   But you're not sure.
ALEX   Not exactly.
POP   The bank manager (7) (want) to see a business plan when you meet her, you know that, don't you?
ALEX   Well, …
POP   Not, 'well'. You need to write down exactly what you (8) (do) and all the figures. The bank (9) (not / lend) you money if they can't be sure that your ideas are OK. Do you want me to help?
ALEX   No … yes, please!
POP   OK, I (10) (come) round to your flat tomorrow or the day after. How would that be?
ALEX   Great! Thanks.
POP   Good. I'm sorry but I have to go now, Alex. My bus (11) (leave) in five minutes.
ALEX   Don't be silly. I (12) (give) you a lift. I've got the car …

1 __are you going to do__

2 _____

3 _____

4 _____

5 _____

6 _____

7 _____

8 _____

9 _____

10 _____

11 _____

12 _____

		1	2	3	4	5	6	7	8	9	10	11	12
a	sicheres Ereignis												
b	Vermutung/Hoffnung/Erwartung												
c	bald eintretendes Ereignis												
d	Plan/Absicht	✔											
e	schon entschiedene Verabredung												
f	spontane Entscheidung												
g	fest terminierter Vorgang (z.B. Fahrplan)												

4 Words!

Translate and write in the missing word or phrase. They were all in this unit of your textbook.

1 Alex is going to call the company Cool Wheels **Limited** . *(GmbH)*

2 The _____ for a new business can be very high. *(Anlaufkosten)*

3 They've got a great idea but no _____ . *(Kapital)*

4 If you do it that way, it will almost certainly _____ . *(schieflaufen)*

5 She has found some people who want to _____ in her project. *(Geld investieren)*

6 The answer is _____ , isn't it? *(eindeutig, völlig klar)*

7 Mr Evans always does what he says he will do. He is very _____ . *(zuverlässig)*

8 You don't think I'm going to do the work _____ , do you? *(umsonst)*

9 If a new business is going to _____ , it will usually happen in the first twelve months.
   (Bankrott machen)

10 So how much do you need to _____ ? *(borgen, sich leihen)*

11 I hear that the bank is going to raise its _____ next week. *(Zinssatz)*

5 Crossword

Complete the crossword.

Across
1 Someone who works with cars.
6 Jeff is Alex's ... .
7 Don't do it later, do it ... !
9 It costs £25. That's a good ... .
12 Twelve months make one ... .
14 Would you like coffee ... tea?
15 Me and you.
16 Money needed to start a business.
17 I am going ... London.
18 Opposite of 'no'.
19 Opposite of 'high'.
21, 15 and 16 down: By using Jeff's cars, Alex won't have any ... .
23 Short form of 'advert'.
24 Possessive pronoun – the dog's bone.
25 'You're late!' 'I'm ... .'

Down
2 Alex ... two people in his garage.
3 Pay to use a car for a few days.
4 'What kind of ... do you have?' 'A Mini.'
5 An old car.
8 You and I.
10 Alex wants to set up a car ... business.
11 The company is called ... Wheels Ltd.
13 Jeff will help Alex with servicing and ... .
15 and 16: See 21 across.
17 Exam.
20 Can you tell me the ... to Jeff's garage?
22 See 17 across.

E The organic food scam

1 Countable and uncountable nouns

Circle the words that are uncountable. You should be able to find 15 more.

(food) ■ specialist ■ health ■ market ■ juice ■ muesli ■ consumer ■ fact ■ price ■

advice ■ dollar ■ bank ■ work ■ job ■ energy ■ information ■ supermarket ■ farmer ■

clothing ■ organization ■ attitude ■ research ■ beef ■ opinion ■ yoghurt ■ example ■

shopper ■ problem ■ the police ■ mile ■ traffic ■ key ■ sugar ■ trick ■ air

2 News, advice, information, etc

Otto had some problems in his last test. Correct his mistakes.

       is   information

1 There ~~are~~ lots of ~~informations~~ in the text about genetically modified *(genetisch verändert)* food.

2 No. The information on the packet in the picture were not correct.

3 All the evidences are that many people today want to eat healthy food.

4 The woman in the shop wanted an advice about the eggs.

5 She had to pay over four dollar fifty for the eggs.

6 The news are not all bad for consumers today, however.

3 Much / many / a lot of (lots of) / loads of / plenty of

Look at the statements below about organic food. Cross out any forms that are not possible. Sometimes more than one form is possible.

1 – So how much / ~~how many~~ is the market in organic food worth every year?

  – I'm not sure. But it must be millions – even billions.

2 Plenty of / A lot of / Loads of people these days buy organic food.

3 That is why so many / so a lot of supermarkets sell it.

4 The market for organic food has grown enormously. Ten years ago, there weren't much / many organic

  products in supermarkets at all. Now the shelves are full of them.

5 Unfortunately, many / a lot of organic food is not really organic.

6 A lot of / Much people don't always have much / many time when they are shopping, so they can't stop to

  think about what they are buying.

7 Many / A lot of people just see 'organic' or 'bio' on the label *(Etikett)* and put the product into their trolley.

8 In fact, though, some 'bio' products contain so much / so many / so loads of additives that they are not really

  different from ordinary, non-organic products.

4 Some / any / something / anything / somebody / anybody / somewhere / anywhere

Charlotte and Joanne share a flat. They are shopping in a supermarket. Complete their conversation with suitable words from the list above.

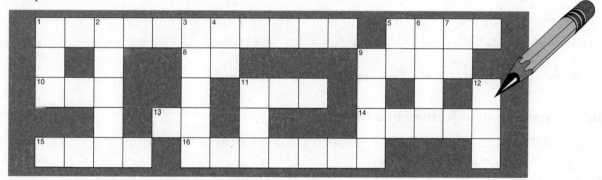

JOANNE   I hate shopping.

CHARLOTTE   Oh, come on, Jo. It's only once a week and it doesn't take long. And we haven't got (1) **anything** at home at the moment. We really need to do this.

JOANNE   OK. Sorry. Right. You get (2) _____ vegetables and I'll go over there and get the pasta. Do you know if we've got (3) _____ spaghetti at home?

CHARLOTTE   You know we haven't. You wanted (4) _____ the other day and there wasn't (5) _____ in the cupboard.

JOANNE   Oh yeah. I'll get (6) _____ spaghetti, then. Would you like (7) _____ tagliatelli, too, if I can find it?

CHARLOTTE   Yeah. Nice idea.

(fifteen minutes later)

JOANNE   So far so good. Now, is there (8) _____ that we haven't got yet?

CHARLOTTE   Yes, we haven't got (9) _____ toothpaste.

JOANNE   I looked for toothpaste a few minutes ago and I couldn't find it (10) _____ .

CHARLOTTE   Well, it must be (11) _____ . Let's ask (12) _____ .

JOANNE   There's never (13) _____ when you need to ask them (14) _____ , is there? Look in the pharmacy and I'll go and stand in the queue at the checkout.

5 Crossword

Complete the crossword.

Across

1 Large, self-service shop wich sells food and often clothes and other goods.
5 Trick to make money.
8 Alison Fox gives her opinion ... organic food.
9 See 9 down.
10 Many people would pay over the ... for 'clean' food.
11 Short for 'biological'.
13 Infinitive of 'am, are, is'.
14 Opposite of 'large'.
15 Where animals live and animal products are made.
16 Food made from milk.

Down

1 Opposite of 'stand'.
2 and 11 down: You can carry things in it (if they aren't too heavy!).
3 You need it to pay for things.
4 Indefinite article.
5 Don't make ... much noise.
6 Fizzy, sweet drink.
7 Short for 'advertisement'.
9 and 9 across: Meals which need little preparation but which are unhealthy.
11 See 2 down.
12 Opposite of 'young'.

F Success starts with S

1 Adjective or adverb?

Cross out the wrong forms.

Mark works in one of the (1) traditional / ~~traditionally~~ service industries: he is a shop assistant. The store where he works is part of a (2) good-known / well-known chain (*Kette*) of Sport and Leisure shops. He has worked there for about eighteen months. The wages are not (3) brilliant / brilliantly, but he hopes (4) eventual / eventually to become a store manager and, as in all careers, you have to start somewhere.

For the first few weeks, Mark found the work (5) extreme / extremely / hard / hardly and at the end of the day got (6) real / really / tired / tiredly. Standing on your feet for eight hours a day is not (7) easy / easily. Saturdays can still seem (8) fair / fairly / hectic / hectically even now.

Retail (*Einzelhandel*) is a service industry and, as in all service industries, you have to be able to get on (9) good / well with people. Mark always tries to say 'hello' (10) friendly / in a friendly way when people come into the store. He also tries to help customers by telling them (11) honest / honestly about the things they are buying. If he thinks that someone doesn't look too (12) good / well in a pair of shorts, he will say so – (13) tactful / tactfully, of course.

There are (14) fortunate / fortunately not many difficult customers, but that's when Mark has to behave (15) particular / particularly / polite / politely. And the store always gives back money – or changes goods – (16) immediate / immediately and without question if there is a problem. As they say, 'the customer is always right'.

2 The comparison of adjectives and adverbs

First fill in the tables, then choose suitable comparative and superlative forms from the tables to complete the sentences on the next page.

ADJECTIVES	COMPARATIVE	SUPERLATIVE
impatient		
exclusive		
easy		
low		
good		
bad		

ADVERBS	COMPARATIVE	SUPERLATIVE
quickly		
efficiently		
long		
fast		
hard		
well		
badly		

1 Some people are a lot **more impatient** than others, aren't they?

2 In restaurants, for example, some people will complain far _____ than others.

3 Some of the _____ people in shops are often elderly people!

4 Kelly is a trainee chef in one of the _____ 5-star restaurants in town.

5 She starts at six every morning and often doesn't finish until midnight. She is the _____-working person I know.

6 Carolyn is the sort of secretary who expects to do everything _____ than everyone else.

7 We stayed at the Royal Swan. It's definitely the _____ hotel I've ever stayed in.

8 Asdi always say in their advertisements that they are the supermarket with the _____ prices.

9 'How much _____ do we have to wait?' he asked at last.

10 – I'm sure I could work these figures out _____ by hand, you know.

  – Well, if you bought yourself a _____ computer you might find it _____ !

3 Word puzzle

Find the words (they were all in this unit) to complete the puzzle.

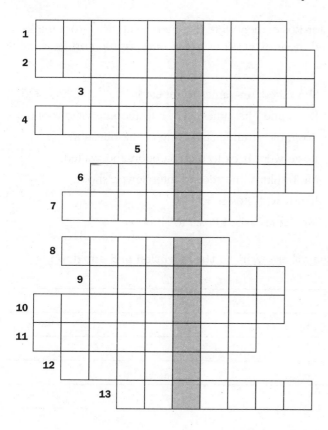

1 Opposite of 'cheap'.
2 Another word for 'often'.
3 When there is not enough of something, there is a ... of it.
4 Someone who believes.
5 Full of life (*lebendig*).
6 On time. Please be ... for the meeting.
7 Superlative of 'lazy'.
8 To say 'no' to something.
9 (Rise/fall) very quickly. Sales rose ... last year.
10 Opposite of 'easy'.
11 A little. Wages could fall ... faster next year.
12 High up in a company; opposite of 'junior'. Mrs Wright is a ... manager.
13 From another country. Could you look after our ... visitor this evening, Mike?

1 Ways into work

1 Past perfect, simple past

Write in the correct tenses of the verbs.

Rosie Lee (1) __was__ (be) really nervous on the day of her interview. After she (2) _____ (have) breakfast and a shower, she (3) _____ _____ (put on) her 'interview clothes' and (4) _____ (catch) the bus into town. The evening before, she (5) _____ (write) down a list of questions to ask at the end of her interview, and on the bus she (6) _____ (read) through these again. Perhaps that's why she (7) _____ (not / notice) the bus stop and (8) _____ (have to) get off a long way from Oxford Laser's office and run back.

Rosie (9) _____ (get) there just in time for the interview. Two other people (10) _____ _____ (already / arrive). Both (11) _____ (look) older than Rosie. One of the others, Julie, (12) _____ (work) in publicity before. 'I'll never get the job,' Rosie (13) _____ (think) quietly to herself ...

2 Past perfect, simple past

Decide the order in which the things happened next for Rosie, then write five more sentences from the list below (A–L) using the past perfect, the simple past and these expressions: *after, once, as soon as, because.* Don't forget the commas.

A   The interview began. ☐

B   <u>Rosie and the others went to the reception and sat down.</u> [2]

C   Rosie's interview finished. ☐

D   Julie had the first interview. ☐

E   <u>All the interviewees arrived.</u> [1]

F   Mrs James came and fetched Rosie. ☐

G   She asked Mrs James to repeat it. ☐

H   Rosie and Mrs James went into the interview room. ☐

I   Rosie didn't understand one of the questions. ☐

J   Rosie went back to the reception and waited. ☐

K   Mr Tomkins, the second interviewer, shook hands with Rosie. ☐

L   Mrs James asked Rosie to sit down. ☐

<u>**Once all the interviewees had arrived, Rosie and the others went to the reception and sat down.**</u>

_____

_____

_____

_____

_____

3 Relative pronouns

Look at the departments in this company and the table and write five more correct sentences.

EXAMPLE

The department which (that) sells the company's products is the sales department.
The person who (that) manages (leitet) ...

ICEBERG FROZEN FOODS LTD

PERSONNEL
Manager: Mrs Rogers

MARKETING
Manager: Mr Tidy

PRODUCTION
Manager: Mr Grant

SALES
Manager: Mrs Clifton

FINANCE
Accountant: Mr Bruce

DISTRIBUTION
Manager: Mr Good

RESEARCH AND DEVELOPMENT
Manager: Dr Susan Richards

The person The department	who which that whose	sells the company's products is the ... department. is the sales manager is called ... . job it is to look after sales is the ... department. manager is Mrs Rogers is the ... department. manages the company's distribution is Mr ... . develops new products is the ... department. name is Tidy looks after marketing. is a 'Dr' is head of R&D.

1 _____

2 _____

3 _____

4 _____

5 _____

4 Wordfield: jobs and employment

1 Find the 'employment' words and phrases (they were all in this unit).

```
JOBS / SKILLSSALARYSECURITYUNEMPLOYMENTOPPORTUNITY
INDUSTRYCREATEMEMBEROFSTAFFUNIONCOMPANYSHIFT
CVLETTEROFAPPLICATIONTEMPORARYPERMANENTEXPERIENCE
QUALIFICATIONSREDUNDANTEMPLOYEREMPLOYEESWAGES
BOSSPAYANDCONDITIONSPERSONNELDEPARTMENT
SHOPASSISTANTMANAGERREPORTERJOBTITLETRAINING
```

2 Now use words and phrases from page 17 to complete the sentences.

a What I like about my company is that they offer plenty of _____ courses, so you can

develop personally and learn new _____ all the time.

b – Where's Mary this evening? – Oh, she's at work. She's working the night _____ this

week.

c – What is Mr Benson's _____ exactly? – I don't know what he does, I'm sorry.

d You really should apply for that job, Sam. It would be a great _____ to work abroad.

e – So, are you working in the production department now then, Mike? – No, the job's only _____

_____ so I can get more _____ . I'll go back to sales again in a week or two.

5 Contact clauses

Complete the missing EU country names and write *who, which* or *that* into the text – but only where
necessary. Put an **X** where you can leave out the pronoun (a contact clause).

Around 10 per cent of all Europeans are unemployed – 16–18 million people. And of those (1) **who** are out

of work, many are young people. The situation (2) **X** we have in Europe today has a number of reasons.

First, people (3) _____ live in countries like China earn much less than workers in, say,

Germany, so the costs (4) _____ firms have there are much lower. This means that the prices

(5) _____ we pay for goods (6) _____ come from Europe are

higher. It is hard for European countries to be competitive.

But aren't there new industries in Europe now, like IT,

(7) _____ can replace the traditional, expensive

ones? Yes, but travelling from one European country in

(8) _____ unemployment is high,

to another where it is lower, is not

always easy. And there are

cultural differences, too,

(9) _____

often make moving

difficult.

The progress *(Fortschritt)*

(10) _____

we have made in Europe

since the EU first began

has been fantastic, but

there is still a lot more

(11) _____

we need to do before we

can say that 'Europe

works'.

Sweden

Northern
Ireland
Scotland

Republic
of Ireland

United
Kingdom

Wales

England

Denmark

The Netherlands

Germany

Luxembourg

Portugal

Italy

Greece

2 Advertising and us

1 The passive: simple present, simple past, will

Complete the text with the best (passive) forms of the verbs.

Advertising is all around us. Billions of dollars (1) **are spent** (spend) every year by companies big and small to promote their products. Sometimes it seems that we, the customers, (2) _____ (bombard) every minute of the day. Advertising is nothing new, of course. No doubt goods (3) _____ (describe) by their sellers as 'the cheapest and best' thousands of years ago. But advertising as we know it today (4) _____ (first / invent) by Americans – people like William Kellogg, Levi Strauss, etc. Among the most popular ads today are those that (5) _____ (watch) every evening on TV. Indeed, it (6) _____ (sometimes / say) that many TV commercials are better than the programmes.

Advertising changes all the time and in the future products (7) _____ (sell) by companies in new ways. You can be sure of one thing, though: the products (8) _____ (still / describe) as the 'cheapest and best'.

2 The passive: present continuous, present perfect

An account executive is sending an e-mail to a client. Put the phrases below into the passive to make it more formal.

1   we have almost completed the work on your campaign
2   we are filming the TV commercial
3   we are printing the posters next week
4   (our space bookers) are making arrangements
5   we have used all of these
6   we are not using cinema ads
7   we are preparing invoices for the posters and filming

Von: adexpert@blastem.uk
Betreff: TV spot

I am pleased to tell you that (1) **the work on your campaign has almost been completed** . The TV commercial (2) _____ at the moment, and the posters (3) _____ _____. Everything will be ready to go in about two weeks. (4) _____ _____ at the moment by our space bookers to place ads in various newspapers and magazines, too. (5) _____ before, and we expect no problems. As we agreed, (6) _____ at the moment, but we can discuss this again when we meet next week. (7) _____ at the moment and will be sent to you soon. Please do not hesitate to contact me if you have any further questions.

3 The passive infinitive after modal verbs

A teacher is explaining the AIDA formula to some business students.
Rewrite the sentences in the passive and add the missing words.

1 First you have to attract the customers' ...

First the customers' ATTENTION has to be attracted.

2 Then we must arouse their ... .

Then _____

3 You could do this with a ...

This _____

4 Next we should create ... for it.

Next _____

5 Finally, we must make ... easy.

Finally _____

6 We may give a ..., for example.

_____ , for example.

7 So, here are the ... again that you mustn't forget.

So, here are the _____

FUNNY PICTURE

ATTENTION

INTEREST

FOUR THINGS

DESIRE

ACTION

FREEPHONE NUMBER

4 Passive questions

Jane has just got a job in an advertising agency and her friend Amy is very interested in how an agency works. Write in her questions.

AMY These people, the 'account executives', they meet the new clients then.

JANE Right.

AMY So (1) **who are the ads designed by?** _____

JANE The ads are designed by the people in the 'creative department'.

AMY Does that take long?

JANE It depends.

AMY I mean, (2) _____

JANE Yes, sometimes lots of ideas are discussed before they find the right one. The idea they decide on finally is called the 'concept'.

AMY Then (3) _____

JANE Yes, then the concept is shown to the client. If they like the idea, then we can produce the ads.

AMY (4) _____

JANE The ads are produced in the production department.

AMY (5) _____

JANE No, the TV commercials aren't produced by us. We use a professional film company for that.

AMY OK. Then what happens?

JANE Then we start putting the ads into newspapers and magazines and on to TV.

AMY (6) _____

JANE That's done by the people in the media department. They're called 'space bookers'.

AMY (7) _____

JANE Of course. Specific ads are always put into specific magazines. For example, ads for expensive cars are put into magazines that are usually read by people who've got plenty of money to buy them!

5 Word building

Who is the person? Fill in the list.

to advertise	**advertiser**	photograph _____	art _____
to produce	_____	to visit _____	science _____
to design	_____	to advise _____	music _____
to write	_____	to sponsor _____	politics _____

6 Wordfield: advertising

1 What sort of advertising can you see here? Pages 41 and 43 in Unit 2 will help you. One sort is not in the book. Invent a name for it.

_____   _____

2 Translate the missing words and phrases.

a Advertising can have many _____ (Ziele).

b Some _____ (vermitteln) information …

c … others _____ (werben für) new products.

d Some adverts try to _____ (überreden) us to buy things we don't need!

e In this ad, the toothpaste doesn't just clean your teeth, it _____ (anbieten) happiness!

f The _____ (Zielgruppe) is teenagers.

g We need to _____ (entwickeln) a new image for the company, I think.

3 There are nine adjectives hidden in the puzzle that could describe advertisements or the things or people in them. Find the words and write them into the lists.

G	X	A	L	T	U	Y	Q	V
S	L	O	V	A	B	L	E	H
H	B	A	D	G	U	C	W	G
O	I	C	M	F	U	N	N	Y
C	X	L	W	O	K	I	T	F
K	R	E	R	E	R	E	T	G
I	Z	V	P	O	E	O	N	M
N	I	E	B	W	V	C	U	X
G	A	R	S	I	L	L	Y	S

POSITIVE	NEGATIVE
_____	_____
_____	_____
_____	_____
_____	_____
_____	_____
_____	_____
_____	_____

1 Conditional sentences type 1

Match the sentence halves.

1 <u>If you send goods by air,</u>

2 Beans from Kenya, for example, will arrive fresh in Europe the same day

3 If you have large, heavy goods that you want to export overseas, however,

4 The big advantage of road transport is that if you send goods by lorry,

5 If you send them by rail,

6 Inside a city, letters and packages will arrive quickest

7 Although if you use some motor bike couriers,

☐ A if you send them by courier.

☐ B you will have to send them by sea, which will be slower but much cheaper.

☐ C they will go straight to the factory or ware-house – it will be a door-to-door service.

☐ D the motor cyclists will probably make lots of car drivers very angry!

☐1 E <u>they will arrive very quickly.</u>

☐ F you will have to transport your goods to and from railway stations.

☐ G if they are sent by air.

2 Conditional sentences types 2 and 3

Continue what these people are saying about different aspects of travel and transport. Put in commas where necessary. Remember: these are all conditional sentences types 2 or 3.

1 RICK (a student): 'If only I had a car!'
If / I / have / car / go / everywhere in it!

If I had a car, I would go everywhere in it!

2 SALLY (a businesswoman): 'Look at this traffic!'
Life / be / so much nicer / if / there / not / be / so many cars on the road!

3 MALCOM BEN (a politician): 'And whose fault is it that our roads are so crowded? The last government's!'
This situation / not / happen / if / they / develop / an integrated transport policy / years ago.

4 MAVIS (aged 103): 'I think all these planes and things they have nowadays are wonderful.'
If / I / have / the chance / when I was young / I / love to travel.

5 HARRY (a businessman): 'I really enjoy travelling on the TGV when I'm in France.'
We / can / have / a much better rail system / in the UK / today / if / we / invest / more money.

3 Unless

Write the phrases under the magazine article into the text using *unless*.

The world is getting smaller, they say. But is it getting slower? Martin Simpson thinks the answer is 'yes'.
YOUR FLIGHT to your sunny holiday resort is 'delayed' – by another five hours. The motorway this morning looks more like a car park than a road. And if you go by train, who knows if you will get there on time!

Travelling really is becoming a nightmare, and (1) _unless we do something about it soon_ , it will get worse. The simple fact is that there are just too many of us on the roads and in the air. It is already difficult to drive anywhere in most of our large cities, and soon it will be impossible (2) _____ to the car problem. And (3) _____

_____, the number of air accidents will increase.

So what is the answer? For many, it is public transport. But buses and trains in this country are not that good. There are hardly any buses any more in the country, so (4) _____ _____, you probably need your car. And (5) _____, _____ we will soon have the worst railway system in Europe.

The world is getting smaller. But (6) _____ _____, life in the 21st century is going to be a lot slower!

1 if we don't do something about it soon	4 if you don't live in a town
2 if we can't find a solution	5 if we don't spend more money on the railways
3 if we don't think carefully about the chaos in the air	6 if we can't find some answers to our traffic problems

4 Connectors

Write connectors from the box into the sentences. More than one answer is often possible.

amazingly	erstaunlicherweise	in addition	zusätzlich
basically	im Grunde genommen	in fact	in Wirklichkeit
last but not least	nicht zuletzt	(un)fortunately	glücklicherweise (leider)
frankly	ehrlich gesagt	moreover	außerdem
generally speaking	im Allgemeinen	nevertheless	trotzdem
however	aber	therefore	daher

1 There was a bad accident on the motorway yesterday. _____ , no one was killed.

2 Everyone is talking about the new by-pass. _____ , I think the idea is stupid!

3 Everyone thought that the telephone would mean that people wouldn't travel any more. _____ , people travelled just as much after the telephone as before it.

4 It has lots of disadvantages, but, _____ , I think most people agree that the car is a wonderful invention.

5 This idea is dangerous. It will pollute the environment. And _____ , it will cost a lot.

6 It's not perfect. _____ , I think it's the best solution we'll find.

7 International trade is terribly important. _____ we need good communications.

8 We cut the tree down. _____ , one of the protesters was sitting in it!

5 Opposites

For each word in Box A, there is one in Box B that means the opposite. Match the words, then use them to complete the sentences below. (Careful: you must make some small changes.)

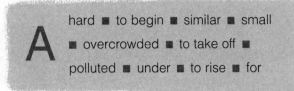

A hard ■ to begin ■ similar ■ small ■ overcrowded ■ to take off ■ polluted ■ under ■ to rise ■ for

B to fall ■ to end ■ easy ■ empty ■ large ■ against ■ over ■ different ■ to land ■ clean

1 No one wants an environment that is **polluted** : we would all like it to be _____ .

2 Some people at the meeting were _____ the by-pass, some _____ it.

3 Production costs have _____ , but transport costs have _____ .

4 It can be _____ to park a car in town, but a scooter is relatively _____ .

5 It was only a _____-scale project, but the costs were the same as for a _____-scale one.

6 The two jobs looked very _____ on paper, but in fact they were quite _____ .

7 You go through the tunnel _____ the river, then _____ the bridge.

8 The programme _____ at 7.30 and _____ at 8.30.

9 The plane _____ at six and _____ at midnight.

10 The roads were all _____ yesterday, but today they are almost _____ .

6 Wordfield: travel and transport

Fill in the crossword. The words were all in this unit.

ACROSS
2 carrying goods from A to B. The firms that carry goods by road are road … firms.
5 to bring (goods) to a customer. We can … your TV tomorrow.
6 every day. There is a … flight.
8 You drive a car but you … a motorbike.
9 (a) something you can eat; (b) a long line of cars that are not moving is a traffic …
10 a short journey to a place and back again, eg a business …

DOWN
1 When you send something on a train you send it by … .
2 (a) the centre of a wheel; (b) the airport at the centre of a network is a … airport
3 what too many cars are bad for
4 a situation, eg at a crossing in a busy city where no cars can move at all
7 what the firms in 2 across use to transport goods

4 *Shop till you drop!*

1 Revision of tenses: simple present, present perfect, will

Fill in the simple present, present perfect or *will* future.

SHOP TILL YOU DROP!

In the last 20 years or so, there (1) **has been** (be) a

shopping revolution.

People today (2) _____ (have) more

money and free time than ever before, and shopping

(3) _____ (become) one of our most

important leisure activities. It (4) _____

(seem) that we (5) _____ (love) to shop till we drop!

Twenty years ago, most stores still closed at around 5.30 or 6 o'clock and at weekends. Since the 90s, this

(6) _____ (change). Shopping malls and high street shops now all (7) _____

(open) much longer hours. There (8) _____ (be) restaurants and cafés in the malls too so

that, for many people, a Saturday or Sunday at the shops (9) _____ (be) a day's holiday.

But shopping in stores (10) _____ (be) still not enough for us! In recent years, technology

(11) _____ (begin) to change shopping, too. Shopping from home (12) _____

(increase), and with the Internet and other possibilities that we (13) _____ (have) in the

future, it (14) _____ probably _____ (become) even more important.

Unless we decide, that is, that shopping (15) _____ (be) boring and we (16) _____

(find) more interesting (and cheaper!) things to do with our time!

2 Retail outlets

Find ten types of retail outlets in the puzzle, then use the words to complete the sentences.

```
M U S I C S T O R E D C O U Q
D L G U T H X X Y M N B Z R K
E W S Y G O V V N H F I R B C
L O T S U P E R M A R K E T F
I D R Q S P O R T S S H O P A
C D E U N I E G E T A A O U S
A Y E R T N N M N Z X H I L H
T W T W Q G V E C J S K L B I
E R M E J M G U R R A H F K O
S X A W W A B Y E U L H S Z N
S I R U S L B N Q T Y J G K S
E I K W A L R B J G I U T X T
N I E A W O M F G I T X M O O
B N T W C U T D O P L M N G R
D E P A R T M E N T S T O R E
```

a   The place to buy your Calvin Klein clothes is a

_____ .

b   A _____ is nice on a sunny

day. Things are often cheaper here.

c   If you wanted trainers or a tennis racket, you could

go to a _____ .

d   Our little _____ sells every-

thing and is open every day.

e   You can get clothes, furniture, TVs, cosmetics, etc at

a _____ .

f   If you need a special cheese or some Spanish saus-

age, you can get them at the _____ .

g   Magazines etc are sold at the _____ .

3 Revision of tenses: simple past, past perfect, past continuous

Lyn and Dave live in the south of England. They often go on shopping trips to Calais, and this is what they did last weekend. Look at the pictures and answer the questions in full sentences.

1 What time did Lyn and Dave get up on Saturday morning?

_____

2 How did they travel to Dover?

_____

3 Did they go to France through the Eurotunnel?

(mit der Fähre – by ferry)

_____

4 What sorts of things did they buy in the big superstore in Calais?

_____

5 What did they do after they had finished their shopping?

_____

6 What happened while they were driving back to the ferry?

_____

7 What did they have to do?

_____

4 Revision of the passive

Greg, a business student, visited a Tesbury's supermarket last week.
The store manager, Tom Head, told him about the company and the store.
Look at what the manager said, and complete Greg's report in the passive.

1 'We built the first Tesbury's supermarket in 1952.'
2 'Since then we have opened another 854 stores all around the country.'
3 'This store first opened in 1995.'
4 'Around 11,000 people use the store every week.'
5 'We are improving the store all the time.'
6 'We have just added *(anbauen)* a new delicatessen.'
7 'At the moment we are making the car park bigger.'
8 'Next month we are changing the decor again.'
9 'We are going to paint the store a nice, fresh green colour.'

The first Tesbury's supermarket (1) __was built__ in 1952, and since then another 854 stores

(2) _____ all around the country. The store that we visited

(3) _____ first _____ in 1995. It (4) _____ by around

11,000 people every week. The store (5) _____ all the time (according

to the manager). A new delicatessen (6) _____ just _____ , and at

the moment the car park (7) _____ bigger. Next month, the decor (8) _____

_____ again. The store (9) _____ green.

5 Translation

Translate these questions.

1 Wann wurde der erste Tesbury's Supermarkt gebaut? __When was the first Tesbury's supermarket built?__

2 Wie viele Geschäfte sind seitdem eröffnet worden?

_____

3 Von wie vielen Leuten wird das Geschäft genutzt?

_____

4 Was ist gerade angebaut worden?

_____

5 Was wird nächsten Monat geändert? (present continuous)

_____

6 Wordfield: shopping

The items on sale in a supermarket can be put into different categories. Choose words from the box and write them under the pictures, then use the words again to complete the sentences.

basic essentials ■ semi-demand items ■ impulse items ■ special offers ■ fresh fruit and vegetables

A   B   C   D   E

_____   _____   _____   _____   _____

1 Things that are non-essential but just nice are called _____ .

2 _____ are things that are sold more cheaply than normal.

3 Things like bread and milk are _____ , things that people need to buy every day. Another word for these is 'demand' items.

4 _____ are things that we need sometimes, but not every day. They are usually placed so that they can be seen easily – and we think: 'Ah yes, I need some spaghetti, too!'

5 _____ are usually placed just inside the store to give a feeling of green, healthy living.

5 *Going global*

1 Indirect statements

This is Enya Kiyonga (textbook page 71). Complete the report about him.

'I'm a farmer near Jinja, Uganda. I grow coffee – nothing but coffee. It's my country's big cash crop: we export it all for foreign currency to buy imports. The trouble is we can't fix our prices. It's those commodity traders in Tokyo, London and New York who do that – non-stop round the world, day and night! And if there's cheaper coffee from, say, Colombia, then our prices go through the floor. A few years ago, I could buy a small truck with my profits. This year I don't have any profits!'

Mr Kiyonga began by saying that that he (1) __was__ a farmer near Jinja, Uganda. He told us that he (2) _____ coffee – nothing but coffee. He said it (3) _____ his country's big cash crop: they (4) _____ it all for foreign currency to buy imports, he said. The trouble (5) _____, he explained, that they (6) _____ fix their prices. He told us that it (7) _____ those commodity traders in Tokyo, London and New York who (8) _____ that – non-stop, day and night. He went on to say that if there (9) _____ cheaper coffee from, say, Colombia, then the prices in his country (10) _____ through the floor. Mr Kiyonga finished by saying that a few years earlier, he (11) _____ to buy a small truck with his profits. That year, he added, he (12) _____ any profits!

2 Indirect requests and instructions

A business class in a British college is doing a project on globalization. Yesterday the teacher gave the students some homework. Write what he said in indirect speech. Use the words in brackets.

1 Look round at home. (want)

   __He wanted them to look__ round at home.

2 Make a list of about ten things manufactured overseas. (instruct)

   _____ of about ten things manufactured overseas.

3 Please bring your list to the next lesson. (ask)

   _____ to the next lesson.

4 Don't bring the things themselves! (tell)

   _____ the things themselves.

5 And don't worry if you can't find ten. (advise)

   _____ if they _____

   find ten.

3 Indirect questions

Later, the students had to contact Nissan's PR department in the north of England. Ann, a student in one of the groups, is reporting to the class. First, she is going through the questions that her group asked. Look at her list and report what she said to the class. Use expressions like: *first, then, next, after that, finally* and *we asked / wanted to know*.

1 How long have Nissan been in the UK?

2 How many people work at the factory?

3 Are the factory managers British or Japanese?

4 Why did you choose Britain for the plant?

5 Where do you sell the cars?

6 How long are you going to stay in the UK?

7 May we have a brochure about Nissan?

First, we asked how long Nissan had been in the UK. Then we wanted to know how _____

_____

_____

_____

_____

_____

_____

4 Reporting verbs

Rewrite the sentences using: *disagreed, thanked, apologized for (x 2), invited, promised (x2)*.

1 'I'm sorry I'm late,' he said.

He **apologized for** being late.

2 'I don't think it's a good idea at all!' Sally told us.

Sally _____ that it was a good idea.

3 'Would you like to visit our factory?' the manager asked.

The manager _____ them to visit the factory.

4 'I'll give you my report tomorrow,' Andy said.

Andy _____ to give his boss his report the next day.

5 'You've helped a lot, Tony. Thanks.'

She _____ Tony for his help.

6 'I regret that I will not be able to come to the meeting,' he wrote.

He _____ not being able to come to the meeting.

7 'I won't tell anyone at all about your problem,' he told them.

Tim _____ not to tell anyone about the problem.

Then write a caption *(Bildunterschrift)* for this cartoon. Use one of the reporting verbs from the exercise.

_____

5 Word building

Fill in the list with nouns from the adjectives or verbs. Use your dictionary if necessary. Then use words from the list to complete the sentences.

to produce	__production__	to explain	_____	to increase	_____
to consume	_____	to inform	_____	to transfer	_____
to solve	_____	competitive	_____	angry	_____
ambitious	_____	to develop	_____	dangerous	_____
to exploit	_____	to manage	_____		
educated	_____	to employ	_____		

1 Parents in poor parts of the world would like more schools where their children can get a good

_____ .

2 With globalization, there is now _____ for jobs and markets all over the world.

3 Many people believe that using children to make footballs cheaply is _____ .

4 The cost of telecommunications has fallen rapidly. As a result, there has been a huge _____

in the amount of _____ that now flows around the world electronically.

5 The young boy in the Indian village was very poor, but very _____ . He wanted to study,

travel and have his own factory one day.

6 There was a lot of _____ when people read the article. A lot of people were angry.

7 I don't think that moving car production to Mexico will _____ our problems!

8 The new Nissan factory brought a lot of _____ to the north of England, where before many

people had been out of work.

9 Of course the _____ of globalization is that people in poor parts of the world get poorer,

while we in the developed countries get richer.

6 Wordfield: globalization

Complete the puzzle.

1 The wool for this shirt came first from Latin America. It came o... from Latin America.

2 You can buy goods from Korea in the EU. Goods from Korea are on ... in the EU.

3 What it costs to do something. Production c... have increased rapidly.

4 The adjective that 'globalization' comes from.

5 When people want to buy goods there is a ... for them. In economics, there is a law of supply and ... .

6 Around the world. The firm operates ... .

7 A big company like IBM that operates in many different countries is a ... company.

8 People working together. The UN and Greenpeace are well-known o...s.

9 Globalization has made the world a smaller ... (Ort).

10 Something that you could have on the Internet. People can look on your ... ... for information. (two words)

11 To bring goods into a country. We ... a lot of our food.

12 Opposite of 11.

13 When you move something from one place to another you ... it. For example, many firms now ... production of their products to the Far East, where costs are lower.

It's all automatic now

1 Articles

Write in *a/an* or *the* where necessary, and translate the highlighted parts into German.

1 Logie Baird (who invented television) was __a__ Scot.   _war Schotte_____

2 James is _____ engineer.   _____

3 What would you like for _____ lunch?   _____

4 They meet about twice _____ year.   _____

5 Send all _____ letters to me.   _____

6 Please take _____ seat.   _____

7 The train leaves in _____ half _____ hour.   _____

8 He's _____ quite _____ nice man, isn't he?   _____

9 Yes, _____ most people think so.   _____

2 Articles

Write in articles where necessary.

RALPH   Morning, Jane. I'm here to see Mr Jackson. Is he in?

JANE   Oh hello, Ralph. Haven't you heard? Mr Jackson has had (1) _____ accident. He's in

(2) _____ hospital.

RALPH   No! When did that happen?

JANE   On (3) _____ Monday. He was coming to work by (4) _____ car and (5) _____ lorry

hit him. He's in (6) _____ new hospital in (7) _____ Queen Street.

RALPH   What (8) _____ pity. I'll go and see him later and take him (9) _____ 'Get Well' card.

3 The definite article

Cross out the sentence in each pair which is not correct.

1 a   Automation has changed all our lives.
   b   ~~The automation has changed all our lives.~~

2 a   Many things that were once done by people are now done by machines and computers.
   b   Many things that were once done by the people are now done by the machines and the computers.

3 a   Many of unskilled people who once did these things are now unemployed.
   b   Many of the unskilled people who once did these things are now unemployed.

4 a   In world in which we live today, it is hard to know where this will lead.
   b   In the world in which we live today, it is hard to know where this will lead.

5 a   We all want to think that life will get better.
   b   We all want to think that the life will get better.

6 a   The life of people in the old car factories was not that good, in fact.
   b   Life of people in the old car factories was not that good, in fact.

7 a   In the future, we all want to enjoy the leisure that IT can give us.
   b   In future, we all want to enjoy leisure that the IT can give us.

4 Participle clauses

Here is an advertisement from the year 2024 for a home computer. Write in -ing or -ed forms which replace the phrases below the advertisement.

Say hello to David!

Did you wake up this morning in a home (1) __filled__ with the sound of music and the smell of hot coffee? Were you late for work because of the traffic? No? Yes? Then you need David, the new intelligent agent (2) _____ by Micro Home, the world's favourite home computer company!

David is for you, someone (3) _____ in today's busy world. David's voice – (4) _____ specially by our engineers – will wake you. He will choose the perfect image to be (5) _____ on your wall, and make sure that the toaster (6) _____ your bread knows just how you like it. And you'll never need to be one of those people (7) _____ in the traffic jams that you see on the way home from work. Having a computer (8) _____ to Trafsat means you'll always know the best way home.

Want to find out more? Then visit our Micro Home website today on Micro Home dot com, or come into one of the hundreds of Micro Home stores (9) _____ around the country. Don't be the person just (10) _____ of a perfect home. Get David – and make your dreams come true!

1	that was filled	6	that toasts
2	which is made	7	who are sitting
3	who lives	8	which is connected
4	which has been developed	9	that are located
5	that will be shown	10	who (just) dreams

5 Participle clauses

Rewrite the two sentences as one using an -ing form and the word(s) in brackets.

1 Jake Dean looked at the figures. He was not happy. (on)

   On looking at the figures, Jake Dean was not happy.

2 His company had automated. It still could not compete with ABC Ltd. (even after)

   _____

3 Then Dave Rogers talked to Jake one day. He explained CIM. (while)

   _____

4 Jake installed a CIM system. He hired some consultants. (before)

   _____

5 They installed the system. They got a big new contract. (a short time after)

   _____

6 The employees at Jake's factory heard the news. They were all really happy. (on)

   _____

6 *-ing* and *-ed* forms as adjectives

Cross out the incorrect word in the captions 1–6 *(Bildunterschriften)*. Then look at the pictures.
Which pictures go with which captions?

1 It was so ~~bored~~ / boring!   C

2 They were very disappointed / disappointing.   ☐

3 You may be a bit surprised / surprising when you see your new office.   ☐

4 Computers can be really annoyed / annoying, can't they?   ☐

5 Jake was very worried / worrying after looking at the figures.   ☐

6 I don't think this film's frightened / frightening at all, do you?   ☐

7 Wordfield: automation

Translate and write in the words in brackets. They were all in the unit.

1 Everything is _____ nowadays. *(automatisch)*

2 Lots of manufacturing industries use _____ processes. *(automatisiert)*

3 This makes them more _____ and _____ . *(effizient / konkurrenzfähig)*

4 The process of looking at a factory and seeing how production can be made more logical and economical is

now called _____ . *(Rationalisierung)*

5 Unfortunately, this sometimes means that managers have to _____ the _____ .

(verkleinern / Personal)

6 Computers can help people in many industries to _____ their various processes.

(koordinieren)

7 A lot of traditional _____ jobs have now disappeared through automation. *(ungelernt)*

8 _____ _____ (or 'IT') is the _____ to the future for

many people. *(Informatik / Schlüssel)*

9 A few years in the future, computers in our intelligent homes may be our _____ to the

outside world. *(Verbindung)*

10 Another word for 'intelligent' is _____ . So you get _____ cards now,

too. *(schlau / schlau)*

7 *The changing world of work*

1 Infinitive or -*ing* form?

Jo has just started working from home – she is a 'teleworker'. Here is part of a letter she has written to a friend. Complete it with the verbs in brackets and the infinitive or -*ing* form. Sometimes, both forms are correct.

... and so at the end of last year, the firm asked all of us if we (1) __wanted to work__ (want / work) from home. We would still be employees of the bank, but we would have our 'offices' in our own home, so to speak.

I thought about it for a couple of weeks, then (2) _____ (decide / say) 'yes'. There were about fourteen of us, I think, mostly women. Well anyway, after Christmas I (3) _____ (begin / work) from here. The bank helped with a computer and a modem. I keep in touch by phone all the time, and go into the office on Fridays.

It's really good, Sue! I have my office in the old guest bedroom and I really (4) _____ _____ (love / be) my own boss. I can work when I (5) _____ _____ (fancy / work) so that means I am always free when Anna and Robert come home from school. I (6) _____ (manage / get) a lot more work done, too. In the office, people (7) _____ (keep on / talk) to you and the phone rang a hundred times a day. Here, it's much quieter. Sometimes I (8) _____ (miss / see) my colleagues, but we meet up again on Fridays, and usually go out for a drink afterwards, so that's OK.

The best part, though, is the travelling – or not travelling! You get up in the morning, have a cup of tea, and you're at work! I always (9) _____ (hate / get up) in the mornings, and I certainly don't (10) _____ (miss / catch) a train into London at 6.30 every day.

Yes, teleworking is for me. It has only been four months, but already I can't (11) _____ _____ (imagine / work) full-time in London again. The bank thinks it is very successful, too, so I (12) _____ (hope / be able) to do this for at least the next three or four years.

That's my news. See you soon.

All the best

Jo

2 Infinitive or -ing form?

Peter Hill and Nina Moss (page 86) are talking about themselves. Three of the underlined phrases have been changed and are (grammatically) wrong. (Circle) the phrases and write them correctly below.

PETER (18)

I'm Peter, and I'm a business student at a college in southern England. I finish my course this summer, then I (1) <u>want to get</u> a job. The thing that interests me most is marketing, and I (2) <u>hope to be able</u> to work in an interesting, modern company. I'm an independent person, so I (3) <u>plan to look for</u> a job where I can do my work in my own way. I couldn't (4) <u>imagine to have</u> a boss who tells me what to do every five minutes!

My name's Nina. A short time ago, my careers teacher (5) <u>suggested to apply</u> for a job with Videocom International and I'm having an interview with them next week. It's a job in the training department. They want a 'team person', and I think that women often (6) <u>seem to be</u> good in teams. I (7) <u>enjoy being</u> with people and I think the work would be interesting. If I got the job, I (8) <u>would like staying</u> with the company for quite a long time.

NINA (19)

☐ _____   ☐ _____   ☐ _____

3 Remember, forget, stop, etc

In each pair of sentences, one sentence needs an infinitive, the other an -ing form. Fill in the correct forms.

1 remember to do / remember doing

   a Remember _____ (turn off) the lights before you leave!

   b Can you remember _____ (see) your college for the first time?

2 forget to do / forget doing

   a I have forgotten _____ (phone) Mrs Edwards. I must do it tomorrow.

   b I'll never forget _____ (take) my driving test – I was so nervous!

3 stop to do / stop doing

   a They stopped _____ (make) steel here many years ago.

   b Just stop _____ (think) for a moment and you'll see that I'm right.

4 regret to do / regret doing

   a Mandy hates her new job and regrets _____ (come) to the firm.

   b We regret _____ (inform) you that Mrs Blackburn no longer works here.

5 mean to do / mean doing

   a It's a great idea, but it would mean _____ (spend) a lot of money.

   b I mean _____ (be) a millionaire by the age of 30!

6 try to do / try doing

   a Have you tried _____ (do) it this way? It is much easier.

   b I can't promise, but I'll try _____ (be) there if I can.

4 Wordfield: the changing world of work

Match these words from the unit and the definitions, then use some of the words to complete the sentences.

1	in-service course (n)	A	Believing strongly in 'masculine' ideas like aggressiveness and strength. A … man.
2	challenge (n)	B	A computer centre where teleworkers can go to use the facilities that they need. There is also a … Association for teleworkers.
3	secure (adj)	C	A training course to learn new skills, etc. It is often paid for by the employer and done by employees during normal working time.
4	macho (adj)	D	Become equal with. Women were once behind men at work but now they are …ing … … them fast.
5	catch up with (v)	E	Something difficult which tests you and which you have to try hard to succeed at. I like new …s.
6	flexible (adj)	F	Able to change, learn new ideas, etc easily.
7	telecottage (n)	G	A … job is one which is safe and likely to last a long time.

1 Our department is going on an _____ course next week to learn the new computer program.

2 Many people believe that _____ ideas at work are now old-fashioned. We need more 'feminine' things like teamwork.

3 Try this. It'll be a bit of a _____ but I'm sure you'll succeed.

4 I love the job but I'm worried that it's not very _____.

5 I'm sure we will _____ our competitors – but we still have a long way to go.

5 Sentence building words

Choose the correct words or phrases from the three possibilities to complete the gaps in the text.

1 because, <u>whereas</u>, although
2 therefore, or, but
3 on the other hand, by contrast, for example
4 also, however, too
5 in fact, despite this, even so
6 while, during, therefore
7 because, and so, too
8 for example, therefore, however
9 firstly, finally, secondly
10 first of all, therefore, moreover

The world of work is changing quickly. One big change is in the kinds of jobs that people do. (1) **Whereas** 50 years ago, many people worked in factories and heavy industries, today, more and more are in high-tech jobs (2) _____ service industries – like finance, (3) _____. Another big change has (4) _____ taken place in the number of women who go out to work. In most families nowadays, both husband and wife have a job. (5) _____, in some families in the future it may even be normal for men to stay at home (6) _____ the woman goes out to work if she has a better job. More jobs are part-time or temporary, (7) _____, these days, which means that many people are spending less time at work that they once did. Part-time work, (8) _____, is not always ideal for people. Firms like the idea, but for employees, part-time jobs are sometimes unsafe or badly paid. (9) _____, there is the fact that some people are now beginning to work from home rather than in an office. One of the big advantages of this is that travel to and from work is no longer necessary and (10) _____ there are fewer cars on the roads.

Eco-disputes

1 Adjectives + prepositions

Write in the prepositions, then use phrases from the list to complete what the two people below are saying. You do not need all the phrases and more than one answer may be possible.

1 afraid **of**	5 fed up _____	9 responsible _____
2 amazed _____	6 interested _____	10 similar _____
3 committed _____	7 keen _____	11 sorry _____
4 enthusiastic _____	8 proud _____	12 worried _____

A 'I think we should all be very (1) _____ what is

happening in the world today. I'm really (2) _____

people who say it doesn't matter! We're all (3) _____

the planet, and we have to try to look after it for our children.'

B 'I wasn't all that (4) _____ the environment until

about two years ago. Then an oil ship sank near where I live on the south coast.

I felt so (5) _____ the seabirds. Now I'm

(6) _____ anything like that ever happening again and

am very (7) _____ making things better. I belong to

Greenpeace, and I'm really (8) _____ what we are doing.'

2 Prepositions of time and place

Jürgen and his friend Bernd have been on an Eco-Tours holiday. Below, you can see the advert that they first saw in an international magazine and part of a letter that Jürgen wrote afterwards to an English-speaking friend. Complete them with prepositions from the box.

> around ■ at ■ from ■ in ■ into ■ on ■ to

Eco-Tours: seeing Kenya's wildlife the natural way ...

With ECO-TOURS you can see some of the most beautiful animals (1) __in__
the world – AND care for the environment.

Fly direct (2) _____ Kenya's capital city, Nairobi. We'll meet you (3) _____ the airport and take you by Landrover
(4) _____ the Treetops Hotel (5) _____ the middle of Kenya's fabulous Serengeti National Park. Our expert
guides take you out each day to see the elephants, lions, and other animals which live free (6) _____ the park.
(7) _____ the morning, wake up to see animals drinking near your window and (8) _____ night, go to sleep with
the sounds of the park all (9) _____ you. It is a holiday that you will never forget.

There are tours every month, and (10) _____ Christmas we organize a special package for people
who want to 'get away (11) _____ it all'.

For up-to-date information about the next Eco-Tour, contact Anita Brown on ...

… We landed (12) _____ Nairobi (13) _____ Monday (14) _____ about 6 pm. One of the guides, Sam, was there with a Landrover. We met the others in our group (15) _____ dinner that night. They were great and came (16) _____ all over the world. Anyway, (17) _____ the morning, we went out with Sam and another guide called Abeli. We drove out (18) _____ the bush, and after about an hour saw a big family of elephants. Sam stopped the Landrover (19) _____ once, and we all got out quietly. I'm sending you a photo. You can see the elephants (20) _____ it. That's Sam (21) _____ the right. It was a great day. We saw all sorts of animals and then drove back. We arrived just (22) _____ time for dinner, then (23) _____ the evening, we sat and talked …

3 Other prepositions

Match the beginnings and ends of the sentences then choose four complete sentences and translate them into German.

1	The Firm is a book by	a	vacation this year, Bernie?
2	Where are you going on	b	the phone to her friends.
3	In other	c	rate, that's what he said.
4	My younger sister is always on	d	John Grisham.
5	Sorry I can't stop. I'm in	e	purpose, didn't you?
6	You did that on	f	words – 'no'!
7	No, I did it by	g	my opinion.
8	Well, he's wrong, in	h	mistake.
9	At any	i	a hurry.

1 _____

2 _____

3 _____

4 _____

4 Prepositional verbs

Complete these sentences about Brent Spar with the correct prepositions.

1 up, about

It is very important that big companies like Shell think **about** *(nachdenken über)* the environment.

2 to, on

The Greenpeace activists went _____ *(weitermachen)* protesting about Brent Spar …

3 off, down

… until Shell had to call _____ *(rückgängig machen)* its first plan to tow it to the Atlantic.

4 through, out

They could not carry the plan _____ *(durchführen)* because public reaction was so strong.

5 for, after, up

So the company looked _____ *(suchen)* a new solution.

5 More prepositional verbs

The <u>underlined</u> phrases in this text can all be rewritten with prepositional verbs from the box.
Which verbs could you use? Write the answers below. Think about the tenses and forms that you need.

(to) give in ■ (to) give up ■ <u>(to) set off</u> ■ (to) turn out ■
(to) turn up ■ (to) work out

In April 1995, Royal Dutch Shell ships (1) <u>began their journey</u> with
Brent Spar out into the Atlantic. And that's when the Greenpeace
boats (2) <u>suddenly arrived.</u>

The takeover of Brent Spar by Greenpeace became big news
across Europe. Public reaction was so strong that some people in
Germany even (3) <u>stopped</u> buying Shell petrol. At the end of June,
Shell (4) <u>stopped fighting.</u> They would not tow Brent Spar to the
Atlantic, they said. They (5) <u>had thought carefully and found</u> a
better idea …

In the end, the situation (6) <u>ended</u> well for the company.
They had shown that a big multinational was ready to listen.

1 <u>set off</u>   3 _____   5 _____
2 _____   4 _____   6 _____

6 Sentence building words

Choose the correct words or phrases from the three possibilities to complete the gaps in the text.

1 surprisingly, <u>naturally</u>, finally
2 in addition, therefore, however
3 despite this, as a result, for instance
4 while, moreover, also
5 hopefully, even so, in fact

6 nevertheless, on the one hand, at last
7 on the other, therefore, whereas
8 last but not least, because, although
9 so, and, but

"Discussions about the environment are never simple! (1) **Naturally**,
we all want to live in a clean and healthy world. (2) _____,
it is not always easy to see how we can best do this. Some people say,
(3) _____, that eco-tourism is a good thing,
(4) _____ others believe that too many tourists are
(5) _____ destroying the environment. We are glad
(6) _____ that big companies like Shell give us petrol for our cars and oil to heat our
homes, but (7) _____ we get very angry when they make a mistake and pollute the sea.
And (8) _____ we think it is terrible that farmers in poor countries clear forests, we have to
understand that this is the only way they can feed their families sometimes. (9) _____ next
time you have an argument about the environment – think carefully before you give an opinion!"

A *Telephoning in business*

Kehler

You are a secretary in the Sales Department of the German company Kehler GmbH, which makes office products like pens, notebooks and mousepads. Your boss, the Export Sales Manager, is Frau Brandt. Kehler export their products all over the EU, including to Britain.

1 Your company telephonist puts a call through to your department. Translate your part of the dialogue.

YOU Verkaufsabteilung. (Ihr Name).

VOICE Oh hello … er … is that the sales department?

YOU Guten Morgen. Ja, hier spricht Frau Brandts Sekretär/in. Mein Name ist (Ihr Name).

_____

MR BELL Thanks. That's better. I can understand now! This is Andrew Bell. I'm the chief buyer *(Chefeinkäufer)* for Martin's the stationers *(Schreibwarenhandlung)* in London. Could I speak to Mrs Brandt, please?

YOU Entschuldigen Sie, wie war der Name noch mal bitte?

_____

MR BELL Bell. B – E – double L. Andrew Bell.

YOU Danke Herr Bell. Es tut mir Leid, Frau Brandt ist im Moment in einer Sitzung. Kann ich ihr etwas ausrichten?

_____

_____

MR BELL That's nice of you, but I really need to speak to her personally. Do you know how long she'll be?

YOU Das ist schwer zu sagen. Oh, Moment mal. Ich glaube die Sitzung ist zu Ende (over). Frau Brandt ist gerade ins Büro zurückgekommen. Ich werde Sie mit ihr verbinden.

_____

_____

2 Choose the best answer. Tick (✔) the boxes.

1 Could you give me your number, please?

  a C – L – A – R – K – E. Clarke. ☐

  b It's four one six double seven eight. ☐

  c Could you hold the line, please? ☐

2 Who's calling, please?

  a Good morning. Sales department. ☐

  b Yes, I've made a note of that. ☐

  c It's Kerstin Willers from Germany. ☐

3 Would you like to call back or should Mr Rogers call you?

  a I'll try again this afternoon perhaps. ☐

  b I'm sorry, he's out of the office today. ☐

  c Can I put you through to somebody else? ☐

4 I'll just check for you.

  a Could you speak more slowly, please? ☐

  b Thanks. ☐

  c My name's Hillebrandt. ☐

5 Thanks a lot for your help.

  a Please. ☐

  b Goodbye. ☐

  c You're welcome. ☐

6 I'm afraid she's speaking on another line.

  a OK. I'll hold the line. ☐

  b Do you know when she will be back? ☐

  c Can you put me through to somebody else who speaks better English? ☐

B *Arranging appointments*

1 You work at the Daimler-Benz Museum in southern Germany, where you are the Museum Director's secretary. The telephone rings. Complete your dialogue with the caller with words and phrases from the box.

> help you ■ mind ■ convenient ■ fine ■ next month ■ What about ■ meet ■ appointments book

YOU	Daimler-Benz Museum. (Ihr Name).
VOICE	I'm sorry, I don't speak German. Would you (1) _____ speaking English, please?
YOU	Of course. I'm the Museum Director's secretary. How can I (2) _____ ?
MS BROWN	Oh, thank you. My name's Jackie Brown. I'm calling from Burley Castle. I'm Lord Burley's personal assistant. Lord Burley has one of the biggest collections *(Sammlungen)* of antique cars in England. He's coming to Germany (3) _____ and he would like to visit your museum and (4) _____ the director. Do you think that would be possible?
YOU	The director would be very pleased to meet Lord Burley too, but I'll have to look in his (5) _____ . One moment, please. So, when is Lord Burley coming to Germany?
MS BROWN	He's coming for three days from the 4th to the 6th of July.
YOU	I'm afraid the director is on holiday on the 4th and 5th. (6) _____ the 6th?
MS BROWN	Yes, the 6th would be (7) _____ . Could we come in the morning?
YOU	Yes, of course. Would 10 o'clock be (8) _____ ?
MS BROWN	Yes, perfect. Thank you. I'll send you a fax next week to confirm the arrangement.
YOU	Thank you. Goodbye.

2 On the morning of Lord Burley's visit, you have to call Ms Brown quickly at her hotel. The clerk puts you through to her room. Translate your part of the dialogue.

MS BROWN	Lord Burley's assistant.
YOU	Guten Morgen Ms Brown. Hier spricht (Ihr Name) vom Daimler-Benz-Museum.

_____

MS BROWN	Oh, hello (Ihr Name). Is everything still all right for our visit?
YOU	Ms Brown, es tut mir sehr Leid, aber ich fürchte, es gibt ein kleines Problem. Der Direktor muss zum Zahnarzt (gehen) Ist es möglich, Ihren Besuch auf 11 Uhr zu verschieben?

_____

_____

MS BROWN	Yes, of course. Thanks for letting me know in time.
YOU	Lord Burley und der Direktor können sich zusammen im Museum umsehen und danach möchte der Direktor Sie und Lord Burley zum Mittagessen einladen (invite … to lunch).

_____

_____

MS BROWN	How very nice of you. Thank you. Lord Burley will be very pleased.
YOU	Gut. Wir freuen uns darauf, Sie dann um elf zu sehen.

_____

MS BROWN	Yes. Goodbye.

FILE C

Making travel arrangements

Harrison Ford is your boss in the Marketing Department of the big American multinational that you work for in Germany. Mr Ford is often away on business trips.

1   Mr Ford has to go to a trade fair in Birmingham, England, next week. Translate your part of the dialogue.

MR FORD   I'd like to make the arrangements for my trip to Birmingham. First I'll need a flight to Birmingham International on Tuesday.

YOU   Zu welcher Zeit möchten Sie in Birmingham sein?

_____

MR FORD   The trade fair begins at 2 pm.

YOU   Also gegen Mittag, wenn möglich.

_____

MR FORD   Yes, that sounds good. Have you booked the hotel in Birmingham yet?

YOU   Ja. Ich habe ein Zimmer für Sie im Birmingham Hilton für Dienstag und Mittwoch reserviert, aber das kann ich ändern, wenn Sie wollen.

_____

_____

MR FORD   No, leave that. That's fine. But I want to stay in England until Saturday now to visit an old friend who lives not far from Birmingham.

YOU   Wie möchten Sie dahin fahren? Soll ich einen Mietwagen für Sie reservieren?

_____

MR FORD   I'm not sure yet. I'll probably take the train, but if I need a hire car I can get one at the airport in Birmingham. There's no need to make any arrangements.

YOU   Und wann möchten Sie Birmingham verlassen?

_____

MR FORD   Early afternoon. I don't want to be back too late.

2   Later that day you go back to Mr Ford with the arrangements. Look at your notes below and complete what you say to him with the missing information. Use the twelve-hour clock, and write out the times in words (eg a quarter to six, nine o'clock, etc).

'I've got your travel arrangements for Birmingham,

Mr Ford. I've booked you onto a BA flight that leaves

(1) _____ on Tuesday morning

at (2) _____ and lands in

Birmingham at (3) _____ local

time. You have a room at the Birmingham Hilton for

Tuesday and (4) _____ night.

I've phoned some car hire companies and, if you decide

to drive to your friend's, you can collect a car at the

(5) _____ itself and give it back at the (6) _____. Then to

come back, it's a (7) _____ flight this time which leaves Birmingham International at

(8) _____. You arrive in Düsseldorf at (9) _____.

> **DIENSTAG 7. MAI** Abflug Düsseldorf mit BA Flugnummer BA 4152 11.30, Ankunft Birmingham International Airport 11.45. Übernachtung im Birmingham Hilton (bestätigt).
> **MITTWOCH 8. MAI** Zweite Nacht im Hilton (bestätigt).
> **SAMSTAG 11. MAI** Abflug Lufthansa Flugnummer LH 298 Birmingham International Airport 13.20, Ankunft Düsseldorf 15.30.
>
> **Mietwagen:** Falls nötig, kann man einen Wagen entweder bei Hertz oder Avis direkt an der Messe mieten und am Flughafen wieder abgeben.

D Making reservations at hotels and restaurants

Next month, some of your managers are going to England for an important meeting with an English firm. It is your job to make the arrangements.

1 The meeting must take place in the week beginning the 18th of April, but the days are flexible. You are phoning a hotel now. Translate your part of the dialogue.

CLERK Good morning. Lakeside Hotel. Tina speaking. How may I help you?

YOU Guten Morgen. Hier spricht (Ihr Name) von der Firma Klaas GmbH in Deutschland. Ich arrangiere gerade eine Sitzung für die Firma und möchte gerne wissen, ob Ihr Konferenzraum für zwei Tage in der Woche vom 18. April frei ist.

_____

_____

CLERK Just a moment. Well, I'm afraid the conference room is booked on Tuesday and Wednesday, but it's available on Thursday and Friday at the moment.

YOU OK. Und haben Sie am Mittwoch, Donnerstag und Freitag fünf Einzelzimmer frei?

_____

CLERK Sorry, I've only got four single rooms available on all those days. But I could let you have one double room at the same price as a single. Would that be OK?

YOU Ja, das wäre sehr gut. Ich habe noch eine Frage. Haben Sie einen Parkplatz am Hotel?

_____

CLERK Yes. Parking is free for guests.

YOU Gut. Dann möchte ich den Konferenzraum und die fünf Zimmer reservieren. Ich werde Ihnen ein Fax schicken, um die Daten usw. zu bestätigen.

_____

CLERK Thank you. Oh, could you just spell your firm's name? Is it C – L – A – double S?

YOU Nein. K – L – A – A – S.

_____

CLERK Fine. I've got all that. I'll look forward to receiving your fax, then. Thank you for calling the Lakeside Hotel. Bye now.

YOU Auf Wiederhören. Und vielen Dank für Ihre Hilfe.

_____

2 The meeting has been very successful, and your firm's managing director wants to go out with everyone to a famous restaurant which is nearby, the Chateau aux Quatre Saisons. You are in England with the team, and they ask you to book a table. Read the notes and write the dialogue. Write your answer on a piece of paper.

Ein Mitarbeiter des Restaurants meldet sich und Sie antworten, dass Sie für heute Abend gegen 19.30 einen Tisch für fünf Personen reservieren möchten. Der Mitarbeiter antwortet, dass sie leider bis Ende Mai völlig ausgebucht (fully booked) sind. Das finden Sie schade. Er teilt Ihnen aber mit, sie hätten ein neues Restaurant, das Bistro aux Quatre Saisons, gerade eröffnet. Das ist nicht weit weg und ist auch hervorragend. Dort werden Sie sicherlich einen Tisch bekommen können. Sie fragen nach der Rufnummer des neuen Restaurants. Der Mitarbeiter gibt Ihnen die Nummer (453871) und Sie bedanken sich.

Arranging meetings and visits to the company

Next week two English clients, Ms Terry and Mr Morrison, are coming over to the advertising agency in Stuttgart where you work as a secretary. Your boss, Martin Schäfer, is presenting a new advertising campaign.

1 The telephonist puts a call through to you. Translate your parts of the dialogue.

YOU DMB und B. (Ihr Name).
SARAH Hello. This is Sarah Osman, Ann Terry's secretary, from Walkers Biscuits in England.
YOU Oh hallo, Sarah. Was kann ich für Sie tun?

_____

SARAH It's about the presentation next week. Mr Morrison's secretary, Mike, has made all the arrangements but now he's off sick! I can't read some of his notes and I wondered if you could help.
YOU Sicher. Einen Moment bitte … OK.

_____

SARAH I know their flight arrives at a quarter past eleven. How are they getting to you from the airport?
YOU Sie nehmen ein Taxi.

_____

SARAH OK. Then what?
YOU Sie essen zu Mittag (have lunch) mit Martin Schäfer hier in der Agentur. Die Präsentation wird um zwei Uhr stattfinden und etwa zwei Stunden dauern.

_____

_____

SARAH Who will be attending the presentation – apart from Mr Schäfer that is?
YOU Zwei Leute aus der Werbeabteilung (creative department) – und eine unserer Designerinnen (designers). Der Direktor, Herr Beckmann, wird auch für die letzte halbe Stunde da sein.

_____

_____

SARAH I know they're flying back straight afterwards. What time do they have to be at the airport?
YOU Gegen halb sechs. Und sie nehmen wieder ein Taxi.

_____

SARAH Great. You've saved my life! Must go now. Bye.

2 It is the day before Ms Terry's and Mr Morrison's visit. Tomorrow, you will have to welcome them at the agency and you decide to note down some useful phrases. Complete the list.

- Ich bin Herrn Schäfers Sekretär/in.   I'm Mr Schäfer's secretary.
- Es freut mich, Sie kennen zu lernen.   It's a pleasure to meet you.
- Hatten Sie einen angenehmen Flug?   _____
- Darf ich Ihre Mäntel nehmen?   _____
- Darf ich Ihnen einen Kaffee oder eine Tasse Tee anbieten?   _____

1 Match the English and German expressions for parts of a letter and say which parts the short extracts from a letter (on the right) are examples of.

letterhead	Unterschriften
date	Empfängeranschrift
reference	Brieftext
inside address	Anlagen
salutation	Briefkopf
subject line	Betreffzeile
body of the letter	Grußformel
complimentary close	Anrede
signature block	Datum
copies	Bezugszeichen
enclosures	Verteiler

a Dear Sir or Madam

   salutation

b 6 June 2001

c Encl: photo

d cc: John Smith

e RS/un

f Thank you for your letter of 16 June in which you …

2 Choose suitable salutations and complimentary closes for the following situations.
There is more than one answer.

a You are writing to David Cooper. He has written you a letter to enquire about your products.
b You are writing to Mason-Sully Inc. It is your first letter to them and you know no one there personally.
c You are writing to Ted Olivetti, a customer that you have known for many years. You use first names.
d You are writing to Rosemary Teller. You met her for the first time last week at a trade fair.

	SALUTATION	COMPLIMENTARY CLOSE
a	_____	_____
b	_____	_____
c	_____	_____
d	_____	_____

3 US Classic Cars want to order a car seat for the de Soto Prestige from Quick Search Automotive Parts Inc. in the States (see the letters on pages 136 and 141 of your textbook). You can see the body of their letter on the next page (page 46 of this workbook). Write in the other parts of the letter with the correct layout. The information below will help you.

REFERENCES	The letter was written by Rolf Schwartz again and typed by Ulrike Nehm.
DATE	The date is 12 July 20.. .
SALUTATION	The letter is to Edward Summers.
SUBJECT LINE	Car seat for 1936 De Soto Prestige
COPIES	A copy of the letter is sent to Markus Redwitz, the Project Manager.
ENCLOSURES	An order form goes with the letter.

US Classic Cars GmbH

Gleiwitzer Straße 23
D- 40233 Düsseldorf

Telefon ++49 (0)211 15 26 37   Telefax ++49 (0)211 15 26 48   E-Mail uscars@aol.de

Your ref/Ihr Zeichen: Our ref/unser Zeichen:

Thank you for your letter of 7 July and the photo.

The car seat looks in good condition and the price of US $1,200 is acceptable.

Please find enclosed our order number 5566/B.

I look forward to receiving the seat as soon as possible.

Enquiries

1 The three people you can see in the pictures are all finding out about a product for the first time. Afterwards, each writes an enquiry to the firm that makes the product. First translate the phrases below, then use them to complete the enquiries A, B or C.

a (Wir) entnehmen Ihrer Anzeige — **(We) note from your advertisement** _____

b (Ich) freue mich darauf, von Ihnen bald zu hören _____

c während / auf der Berliner Messe _____

d Sie wurden uns von einem Kunden empfohlen _____

e Würden Sie bitte veranlassen, dass Ihr Vertreter uns besucht _____

f ein führender Importeur _____

g Preisliste _____

h Handelsrabatte _____

i (es gibt) einen wachsenden Markt _____

j Danke im Voraus für Ihre Hilfe _____

k Gegenwärtig erweitern wir unser Sortiment von _____

A When I visited your stand (1) _____ , I was interested to see that you are a supplier of 'environmentally friendly' garden furniture. We are (2) _____ of garden furniture in the UK and I am therefore interested in finding out more about your products. Please send us your current catalogue and (3) _____ . I (4) _____ .

B We (5) **note from your advertisement** in this month's European Retail Magazine that you can supply a wide range of French jams and fruit conserves. There is (6) _____ for products like these in Germany and, as the country's largest food retailer, we would like to find out more about your range. (7) _____ at our head office here in Dortmund? I hope to hear from you shortly.

C (8) _____ who also gave us your address. (9) _____ _____ cosmetics, and feel that your products would fit well *(gut hineinpassen)*. Please send us your current catalogue and price list. Could you also please send us information on (10) _____ _____ and delivery periods? (11) _____ . We look forward to hearing from you in due course.

2 Herr Völker (the owner of Völker Sporttechnik GmbH in Essen) is angry because someone has written this letter for him – and it is full of mistakes. Herr Völker has circled the problems and gives the letter to you to correct. Write the correct English below.

Gold Medal Sportswear Ltd

43 Princes Road

Milton Keynes MK3 2NW

England

19. 2. 20 . .

Dear Sir or Madam

Enquiry

(1) we obtained your (2) adress from your Internet site and understand that you are (3) supplyers of sports clothes, like T-shirts, shorts and trainers.

We are a (4) german wholesaler of sports equipment and supply sports goods to retailers throughout Germany.

Please send us your current catalogue and price list for your sports (5) clothies. We would also be (6) greatful for (7) informations on trade discounts and delivery periods.

Thank you in advance for your help. We look forward (8) to hear from you (9) in short.

(10) Yours sincerely

Völker Sporttechnik GmbH

Jens Völker

Jens Völker
Chief executive

1 **We** _____ 6 _____

2 _____ 7 _____

3 _____ 8 _____

4 _____ 9 _____

5 _____ 10 _____

3 Here is part of an enquiry that Völker Sporttechnik has received. Translate the e-mail into German.

We are a large British company which is planning to open a new office in Essen later this year. We want to install a Fitness Centre in our office for our employees and we are currently writing around to suppliers of sports equipment in the Essen area. Could you please send us a brochure about your company, five catalogues and a price list? Thank you in advance for your assistance.

_____

_____

_____

_____

_____

_____

_____

_____

_____

_____

1 Complete the offer with words and expressions from the box.

EUR 150 ■ Payment ■ Export Sales ■ enquiry ■ DDP ■ interest ■ questions ■
quotation ■ trade discount ■ valid ■ immediately

Dear Mr Kleine-Horst

With reference to your (1) _____ of 15 September, we have pleasure in

submitting the following (2) _____ .

1	25 x	Woodland garden chairs		EUR 2500
2	5 x	Woodland garden tables		EUR 600
3	2 x	'Happy Bird' bird tables		(3) _____

All prices are (4) _____ .

We are pleased to offer you a (5) _____ of 8% off list price.

(6) _____ should be within 30 days of delivery.

We will send the goods by road transport (7) _____ on receipt of your order.

This offer is (8) _____ for three months from the above date.

Thank you for your (9) _____ , and we look forward to receiving your order.

If you have any (10) _____ , please do not hesitate to get in touch.

Yours sincerely
Woodland Garden Products Ltd

Sandra Lewis

Sandra Lewis

(11) _____

2 Sandra Lewis could have used other expressions in her letter. Match the phrases she used (on the left) with those (on the right) that would have had the same or a similar meaning.

1	With reference to …	A	The consignment will be dispatched …
2	we have pleasure in submitting …	B	The offer is firm …
3	We are pleased to offer you …	C	We refer to …
4	We will send you the goods …	D	we are pleased to send you …
5	This offer is valid …	E	Should you require further information …
6	If you have any questions …	F	please contact me
7	please do not hesitate to get in touch	G	We are willing to allow you …

3 A colleague who works in your office is not very sure of her English and often asks you to check her letters. This week she has written a number of offers. Help her by choosing the correct words and expressions. Circle the correct forms.

1 Thank you for your letter (of) / from 2 February.

2 With reference to / on / about your enquiry.

3 We have pleasure to submit / in submitting …

4 We are pleased sending / to send you the following …

5 We can give you a trade discount of 10% off / by / under the list price.

6 Payment should be made on / at / with receipt of the goods.

7 Please pay through / by / over irrevocable letter of credit.

8 The consignment will be sent over / by / per air.

9 We are certain that you will be happy for / over / with our product.

10 We look forward to recieve / to recieving / to receive / to receiving your order.

11 If you have any questions, please get in / on / into touch with me.

4 Your company has received the following important offer and your boss asks you to translate it into German so that she is sure of all the details. Write out your translation.

Thank you for your phone call last Tuesday about our blank cassettes *(Leerkassetten)*. Enclosed you will find our current price list, plus the CIF Hamburg prices which I have worked out for you.
As you will see, we are pleased to offer you a volume discount of 12.5% if you order more than 10,000 cassettes. Payment should be by irrevocable letter of credit. Large orders of cassettes will be dispatched to you by sea from Hong Kong and you can expect to receive them approximately six weeks after we get your order. This offer is valid for six months from the date of this letter.
Thank you for your interest. We are certain you will be delighted with our product and look forward to doing business with you in the future.

_____

_____

_____

_____

_____

_____

_____

_____

_____

_____

_____

_____

FILE

4 *Orders and acknowledgements of orders*

1 Hidden in the puzzle are ten words that you might use in an order. Find the words, then use them to complete the order below.

A	C	C	E	P	T	A	N	C	E	U
Q	C	H	E	Q	U	E	P	N	M	Y
Q	D	K	N	C	H	F	T	E	R	Z
U	E	B	N	S	W	I	T	H	I	N
O	L	D	E	O	W	N	H	L	K	A
T	I	F	F	R	W	C	Z	X	K	P
A	V	E	E	J	J	L	W	U	B	L
T	E	D	Q	J	H	U	E	C	C	A
I	R	L	M	F	E	D	S	D	S	C
O	Y	W	G	I	A	E	B	V	G	E
N	T	V	B	D	U	X	T	K	I	E

Computer Fun GmbH

Kiefholzstraße 119
D–12437 Berlin

Computer Games Ltd.
Hampton Trading Estate
11–13 Works Road
Hampton TW12 3ED
GB – Middlesex

Dear Mr Richardson

Many thanks for your (1) _____ of 18 June. We would like to (2) _____

the following (3) _____ for computer games:

1	10 x 'Masked Raider'	EUR 240
2	10 x 'Space Invasion II'	EUR 240
3	15 x 'Wildlife Safari'	EUR 300

We understand that these prices (4) _____ a discount of 8%.

Payment: by (5) _____ within 30 days of delivery.

(6) _____: by road DDP our Solingen store (7) _____ 7 days

of receipt of this order.

Please (8) _____ your (9) _____ of this order

immediately by (10) _____.

Yours sincerely
Computer Fun GmbH

Claudia Schubert

Claudia Schubert
Purchasing Assistant

Encl: Order No 100 1024

2 Mr Richardson sends Ms Schubert a fax to confirm her order but makes six rather important mistakes. She corrects these on the fax and sends it straight back to Mr Richardson. Find and correct the other five mistakes.

Dear Ms ~~Beethoven~~ — *Schubert*

I acknowledge receipt of your order no. 100 1024 and confirm the details contained in it, as follows:

1	10 x 'Masked Raider'	EUR 240
2	10 x 'Space Invasion III'	EUR 240
3	10 x 'Wildlife Safari'	EUR 300

We confirm that these prices include a discount of 8%. The consignment will be dispatched by road DDP your Bochum store within two weeks of receipt of order.

Please note that payment must be made in advance.

Thanks again for your order. We are certain you will be fully satisfied with the games which are extremely popular in this country.

Yours sincerely

Archie Richardson

3 Complete the table. Then use some of the words to complete the sentences.

ADJECTIVE	VERB	NOUN
acceptable	(to) accept	*acceptance*
–	(to) acknowledge	
–	_____	receipt
–	_____	quotation
_____	(to) introduce	introduction
–	(to) pay	_____
–	(to) deliver	_____
–	_____	expectation
–	_____	confirmation
satisfied / satisfactory	_____	satisfaction
–	(to) delay	_____
–	(to) offer	_____
–	_____	enquiry

1 Thank you for the prices that you quoted. Thank you for your _____ .

2 You must pay within 30 days. _____ must be within 30 days.

3 The goods were delayed. There was a _____ with the goods.

4 We can give you a discount as an introduction. We can give you an _____ discount.

5 The products were as good as we had expected. They came up to our _____s.

6 Please pay as soon as you receive the order. Please pay on _____ of the order.

7 Sorry, we cannot accept your terms of payment. Your terms of payment are un_____ .

8 The people who bought the games found them satisfactory. They were very _____ with them.

9 Can you write an enquiry about prices? Can you write and _____ about prices?

10 They must send us an acknowledgement of our order. They must _____ our order.

1 Gerd Lorenz works at the exclusive Café Klausewitz on Berlin's Unter den Linden. He is the café manager's secretary. Gerd's boss wants him to write to an English firm in Stafford about some tea cups which have not arrived. Look at the café manager's notes and complete Gerd's letter with suitable words and phrases.

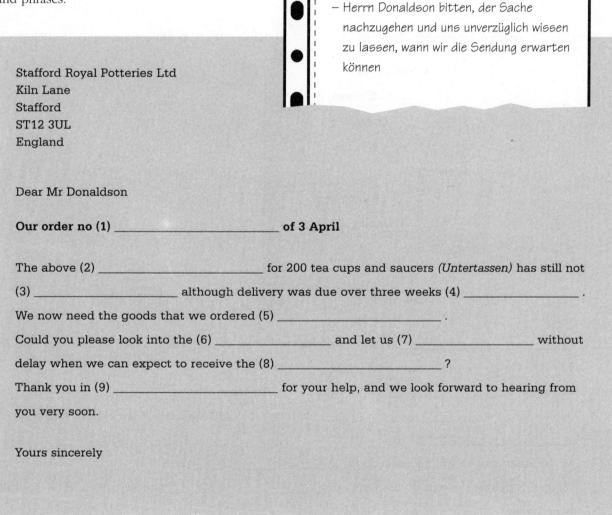

– Bestellung (Nr. 95826 v. 3. 4.) für Tee-tassen immer noch nicht angekommen

– vereinbarter Liefertermin vor drei Wochen, d.h. 28. 4.

– Betonen: wir brauchen die Tassen jetzt dringend

– Herrn Donaldson bitten, der Sache nachzugehen und uns unverzüglich wissen zu lassen, wann wir die Sendung erwarten können

Stafford Royal Potteries Ltd
Kiln Lane
Stafford
ST12 3UL
England

Dear Mr Donaldson

Our order no (1) _____ **of 3 April**

The above (2) _____ for 200 tea cups and saucers (*Untertassen*) has still not

(3) _____ although delivery was due over three weeks (4) _____ .

We now need the goods that we ordered (5) _____ .

Could you please look into the (6) _____ and let us (7) _____ without

delay when we can expect to receive the (8) _____ ?

Thank you in (9) _____ for your help, and we look forward to hearing from

you very soon.

Yours sincerely

2 Gerd has now received the tea cups from England, but there is still a problem. He sends the e-mail (next page) to Mr Donaldson. Put the lines of the text in the right order, then find the words and expressions that mean the following:

1   another carton instead of the damaged one   **_a replacement carton_**

2   inform us _____

3   so that you will have to pay the costs _____

4   sending them back _____

5   are so damaged _____

6   confirm that we have received _____

7   the individual goods _____

3 Translate the German expressions, then use some of the English ones to complete the sentences below.

```
 1 Spezifikation          ☐☐☐■☐☐☐☐☐☐☐☐☐
 2 Waren                  ☐☐■☐☐
 3 sofortig               ☐☐■☐☐☐☐
 4 hoffen                 ☐☐■☐
 5 mehrere     ☐☐☐☐☐■
 6 stornieren             ■☐☐☐
 7 Haltung                ☐☐■☐☐☐
 8 auf dem Transportweg (2 words) ☐☐☐☐■☐☐☐
 9 bedauern               ☐☐☐■☐
10 Sendung                ☐☐☐■☐☐☐☐☐☐
```

1 We _____ to inform you that our order number AA/224 has not yet been delivered although it was due within six weeks.

2 We expect the _____ delivery of the missing items.

3 On checking the _____ , we found that all the glasses in the cartons had been broken _____ .

4 We are sure that you will understand our _____ .

5 The goods that you sent us do not meet our _____ and we are therefore returning them to you.

6 Because of all the problems that we have had over the last six weeks, and because the replacements have still not arrived, we wish to _____ our order.

4 You have received this rather angry e-mail from a client in the US and your boss wants to know what it means. Translate into German.

> Two months ago we ordered a large consignment of clocks and watches from your company. The delivery of the goods was very slow but they finally arrived this morning. Now on checking the order I find that it is incomplete because six of the clocks are missing. Our customers are waiting for the clocks and I cannot keep on telling them that the clocks are 'on the way'! Please send us the clocks (order numbers below) without delay.

1 The <u>underlined</u> parts in this first reminder are all in the wrong places in the letter. Write out the reminder again correctly.

> <u>Yours sincerely</u>
>
> We refer to the enclosed invoice of 19 October <u>been overlooked or mislaid</u>.
>
> As we are certain that it has simply <u>which is still outstanding</u>, we would be pleased if you could <u>ignore this reminder</u>.
>
> <u>within 30 days</u> in our acknowledgement of order, invoices should be paid <u>As stated</u> of receipt of goods.
>
> If you have paid the invoice in the meantime, please <u>settle it as soon as possible</u>.
>
> <u>Dear Ms Olivetti</u>
>
> Uta Hübner
> Customer Accounts

_____

_____

_____

_____

_____

_____

_____

_____

_____

2 Match the German and English phrases, then use six of the English expressions to complete the second reminder on the next page.

1	mit Bezug auf	A	in accordance with
2	wir haben immer noch keine Zahlung erhalten	B	further to
3	entsprechend	C	in order
4	die Rechnung begleichen	D	to insist on
5	es wird nicht nötig sein	E	we have still not received payment
6	setzen Sie sich bitte mit mir in Verbindung	F	to settle the invoice
7	in Ordnung	G	a final opportunity
8	von Ihrer Bank fehlgeleitet worden ist	H	please get in touch with me
9	bestehen auf	I	has been misdirected by your bank
10	eine letzte Möglichkeit	J	it will not be necessary

Dear Ms Olivetti

Our invoice no 1225/A/23 of 19 October

(1) _____ our reminder of 1 December 20.., we are surprised that

(2) _____ for the above invoice. The order was carried out

(3) _____ your wishes and the consignment was delivered on the date agreed.

We must, therefore, ask you (4) _____ by 8 December at the latest.

We look forward to receiving payment and are sure that (5) _____ to write to you

again. If there is a problem that I should know about, (6) _____ at once.

Yours sincerely

Uta Hübner
Customer accounts

---

3 Your colleague at work has had some problems with a letter again. Help him to choose the correct forms in the sentences below. Circle the correct forms.

1   Further to / at our reminder of / from 30 January …

2   Payment should be made by / on / at delivery.

3   The consignment was delivered as agreed on / in the 14 November.

4   As we have received no complaint from you, we must assume / assure that the consignment was in order …

5   … and it was with / to / under your satisfaction.

6   Could you please let us have / let you have / have you let us your payment within the next few days.

7   If we have not received payment in full within 7 days, we will put the matter in / onto / into the hands of our lawyers.

8   Perhaps the enclosed invoice has been overlooked / overseen by you.

---

4 Complete the puzzle. All the words have to do with reminders.

1   The document that you have to remind people about when it has not been paid.

2   *Frist*

3/4   *paar Tage.* Please pay within the next … … (3 letters/4 letters).

5/6   immediately, *sofort.* Please let us have your payment … … (2 letters/4 letters).

7   *überrascht.* We are … that you have still not paid.

8   (of invoice) not paid yet, *ausstehend*

9   *Zustand.* The goods arrived in good … .

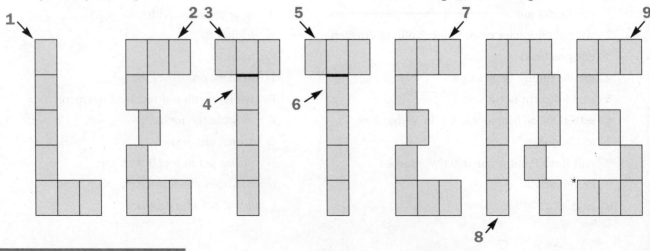